9 HEROIC STRATEGIES TO IGNITE
THE BEST VERSION OF YOU

MAKE
FEAR
YOUR
SUPER
POWER

DR. TAMEKA FERGUSON

Published by Entirety Inc. Publishing

Praise for

"MAKE FEAR YOUR SUPERPOWER"

Thank you, Tameka Ellington, for these insights, gems and nuggets of brilliance. You have put your heart, time and soul into this important book. I was not only informed and inspired but empowered by your words and ideas on this critical subject of "Fear," particularly in the Black community. I wish I knew the 9 Heroic Strategies in *Make Fear Your Superpower* when I was growing up. You have the answers and solutions, and they are precise, timely and needed. Bravo! We all now have something worth reading on this critical subject that directly addresses the many fears of African Americans but when read, can benefit everyone. Thank you so much for this empowering gift.

—Dr. George C. Fraser

Chair and CEO of FraserNet, Inc.,
Author, *Success Runs In Our Race, CLICK and Mission Unstoppable*

In her new memoir, Dr. Ellington becomes the HERO of her own story, by summoning the courage to face the fear and do it anyway. Her story will inspire, encourage, and challenge anyone who thinks it is too late to become the person you are meant to be.

—Dr. Angela Neal-Barnett,
Internationally Renowned Psychologist and
Author, *Soothe Your Nerves: The Black Woman's Guide to Overcome Anxiety, Panic and Fear*

I stand in awe of Dr Tameka Ellington's honesty, determination and courage to share her experiences to transform what could be a debilitating struggle into an uplifting, motivational message to help others. Her dedication and commitment to family, teaching, creativity and helping others is clearly what drives her passion.

—Sharlene Ramos Chesnes,
President and CEO of The InterChez Companies

WOW! Dr. Tameka N. Ellington has written a powerful self-help, transformation manual for all ages, personal aspirations and individual levels of education, training and expertise. Make Fear Your Superpower allows the reader to look behind the scenes and go into the mind of a courageous warrior that has been both motivated and willing to face her fears and continually step out in new directions to challenge and overcome them. Make Fear Your Superpower is a must read for any person - especially females - seeking a role model and 'G.P.S.' to guide their steps towards transformation and liberation. We all owe a great debt to Tameka for her courage and willingness to face the 'slings and arrows' necessary to bring us these powerful insights and life lessons.

—Dr. Kwa David Whitaker, Esquire a.k.a.
Nana Kra Kwamina,
Lawyer and Educational Psychologist,
U.S.A. born Chief of the Akan tribe in Ghana
Author, *Why I became an African Chief*

DEDICATION

As I reflect on the process of writing this book, my first book. I have always been a writer and storyteller since I was a child, so the words flowed freely from me most of the time. But then came those times of blockage, times when I just didn't know how to put my thoughts on the page. In those moments God showed up in ways that I could not have imaged he would. Ideas for Make Fear Your Superpower came from multiple consciousnesses; while I was wide awake, while I was meditating, while I was dreaming, while I was reading or watching powerful videos, and even in mid-conversation with family and friends. God, all my gifts come from you! I am so grateful that you have given me this platform to share my story and uplift others.

ACKNOWLEDGEMENTS
WITH ALL MY LOVE!

Tabitha Messmore, my editor and one of my entrepreneurial mentors, thank you for trudging through the drafts and helping me make sense of formulating Entirety Incorporated into a reality. You have been awesome to work with and I look forward to our next go round!

My students, over the past 14 years I've had the honor of educating hundreds of students. I have come to know many of you very well, and some of you have become a major part of my life. Because of you, I was able to get through the turmoil that comes with being the first African American professor at the Kent State University Fashion School. When times got tough, I thought of you and the joy I get it from being with you in class and working with you on research. You inspired me to be a better educator and mentor.

The Intrepid 9, we experienced voyaging to Ghana West Africa together. We learned so much about our ancestors and the experience that I had with you is unexplainable with words. It is a feeling that I will never ever forget. You will always hold a special place in my heart. .

Baba Mwatabu Okantah thank you for welcoming me into the Intrepid 9. It has been a pleasure getting to know you as my professor when I was in undergraduate to now being your peer and colleague. Thanks for all the knowledge you dropped over the years and thanks for introducing me to Chief Kwa David Whitaker a.k.a. Nana, who shared with us his love and knowledge of Ghana.

Nana, you are a perfect example of how tightly connected our world really is. During our time in Ghana, I had mentioned wanting to meet Dr. George Fraser (someone I had been following via his books and video lecturers) and Nana just so happened to be one of his best friends. Thank you, for your wisdom, realness and of course, thank you for introducing me to Dr. Fraser. I'm striving to be like you both—living life in an abundant way.

Dr. George Fraser, you are an inspiration to me as I begin my entrepreneurial journey. Meeting you makes the work real and attainable. Thank you for being an amazing role model. I look forward to working with you and learning from you.

I've been blessed with several mentors over the years. Your guidance and knowledge helped catapult me to where I am today and I am so grateful! Some mentors were there just as a word of advice, somewhere there as a shoulder to cry on, and others were there as a shining example of what success looks like.

Sharlene Chesnes, my mentor, you have been all those to me. As an amazingly brilliant woman of color who is a successful entrepreneur, fellow Clevelander, fellow Trio alum, a first-generation revolutionary, my birthday twin and one of the kindest people I know, you are an exemplary model that success is for everyone, no matter where you begin in life.

Dr. Linda Angotti, my mentor and fellow arts faculty, thank you for helping me navigate through my tenure and promotion process and for being a glimmer of light when I needed it most.

Dr. Angela Neal-Barnett, my mentor, you have changed the lives of many, many African American women with your Rise Sally Rise movement and all the work you have done with anxiety disorders. You have ALWAYS been an advocate for me from the first day we met, I love you and appreciate you for that.

Dr. George Garrison and Dr. Christopher Williams, you are the reason why I was able to break the barrier and become the first African American Professor in the Fashion School at Kent State University. The strength and support you have given to so many faculty of color is immeasurable! You and the "team" kept our small subculture going and you consistently held administration responsible for diversity matters at our university.

Dr. S., my therapist, you have changed my life and helped me stay focused on being a Christian woman, wife and mother. Your continued encouragement has given me the superpower to come into my entrepreneurial strength.

Dr. Sonya Wisdom and Dr. Keith Wisdom, my visionaries, you saw something in me that I could not have ever known was there until I continued to seek and own up to what God was calling me to do.

Malia Mast, thanks for expanding my library. You saw the vision before I did.

Cory Wallace, my brother and one of my oldest friends, I've been fortunate to see you grow from a young man just trying to make it out of the inner city of Cleveland to becoming a Navy Captain. I am so happy that I have you to continue on our journey of friendship as well as this new journey of entrepreneurship. I look forward to our forever friendship.

Nickole Holms, my sister and one of my newest friends. You were the best thing that came out of my Jack and Jill experience! I greatly appreciate the laughs and for you allowing me to cry when I needed to. I look forward to walking the entrepreneurial journey with you. Thank you for allowing me to hold you accountable to your dreams and goals and for you doing the same for me.

My godmother, Tammi Cava, thank you for your love and for helping to guide me along my spiritual journey. I'm so grateful to you for introducing me to the world of reiki and inner consciousness. I look forward to learning more from you.

My ex-business partner and friend, Joy King, thank you for helping me get the guts to start my entrepreneurial journey. Even though things didn't work out with us going into business together, what I learned about myself in the process, will allow me to take my future to the next level.

My baby sister, Tasha Ferguson, I have enjoyed growing up with you! You know me better than almost anyone in the world. You witnessed the heart ache and the joy and now I want you to witness our family being lifted from our generational curse of poverty. We can do this, and I want you by my side all the way!!

My brother, Mardy Ferguson, you are one of the special men in my life. I'm so proud of where you have come, and I want to challenge you to go further. You are a great dad and I'm proud of you for staying in your children's life. They need you, just like we needed our dad. We started from the bottom, but we don't deserve to stay there. You are amazing and I can't wait to continue to see you grow.

My dad, Mardy Reeves, words cannot describe how proud I am of you. You could have easily crawled back into the trap of addiction, but you didn't; because you saw the value in staying connected with your family. Your time away from us was very hard. There were so many things that you missed. I am so happy that you stayed on the straight and narrow so that we can get to know you better and continue to build our relationship with you.

My mom, Pamela Ferguson, you are a blessing to me. My relationship with you shaped who I am today. We've had our ups and downs, but I'm so grateful that we have figured out a way to love each other and become better friends. My entire existence was to make you proud of me. It was so hard for me when you didn't see it that way. I'm blessed that God gave us a second chance and now I live to take care of you.

My husband, Dr. Aaron Ellington, thank you for loving me when I was not loveable and for always being in my corner no matter what. You have helped transformed me into the woman I am today. I've learned so much from you and I want to thank you for always being an amazing model of what a "good man" looks like.

My boys, Aaron Jr., Xavier and Maxwell—you are why I breathe! I am building a legacy for you to carry on for generations to come. Poverty is our past, it is not who we are. It takes only one moment to decided that you want something different in your life, but it takes the rest of your life to stay on the path to attain it. Always aim for excellence in everything you do, be good to others, love each other always and remember who sent you and why you were sent here. Your journey to discovering your SUPERPOWERS has just begun!

9 HEROIC STRATEGIES TO IGNITE
THE BEST VERSION OF YOU

MAKE
FEAR
YOUR
SUPER
POWER

DR. TAMEKA ELLINGTON

TABLE OF CONTENTS

INTRODUCTION
A DEFINITION OF FEAR

Every year entrepreneurs, artists, leaders, innovators, and visionaries gather at mind, body, spirt wellness festival hosted by Mindvalley—A-Fest. During an interview at the 2016 A-Fest, transformational speaker and entrepreneur, Lisa Nichols refers to the word FEAR as an acronym for False Evidence Appearing Real. Basically, fear is something we make up in our heads—a mental psych-out that fools us into believing circumstances that have not and may not happen. Fear makes us feel weak and uncertain. We're not born with it; fear is a learned state of being. Fear is debilitating and paralyzing. Fear will keep us from the careers, love relationships and adventures that we have dreamed of. Our fearful thoughts can take control of our bodies and actions if we let them. Fear only has the power that we give it.

"Our emotions have a vibratory
frequency of them
There are only two emotions that

mankind experience: fear and love
While other emotions branch either
directly or indirectly from these two
emotions
Fear has a long and slow frequency
vibration to it while love has a very rapid
and high frequency."

These are the lyrics to singer/songwriter, Erykah Badu's ballad, "Love." In this verse, Badu is explaining the paradox between fear and love and how one can't exist when the other is in motion. We can't be truly happy for someone, if deep down we are jealous of that person. She said it best in a 2017 Aftopunk.com interview, "Fear is the opposite of love. Love looks like kindness, compassion, patience, forgiveness. Fear looks like jealousy, being in competition, being hateful, and envy. The two can't occupy the same space at the same time."

The type of fear that this book will address is a much deeper form of fear. Not the surface fears such as fear of heights or fear of a scary movie; but a fear of our human selves and our potential and capacity for success. A fear that manifests itself into self-hate and self-doubt.

Michelle Obama, former United States First Lady, stated "Don't ever make decisions based on fear. Make decisions based on hope and possibility." Hope and possibility means that we have a chance at success. Just like love, fear is the opposite of what we would refer to as hope or faith. Faith is hope with a bit of the Lord Jesus sprinkled on top. If we have hope or faith, ANYTHING we can imagine is possible. Without hope or faith, those thoughts are just daydreams that will lay stagnate in our minds.

For an Afrocentricity perspective on fear, we must look back at our history. Africans were smuggled into this country shackled and stacked. They were scattered throughout the Diaspora under cruel conditions of fear. Therefore, African Americans and others of African descent throughout the world have much more work to do than our non-African sisters and brothers in order to reverse and un-brainwash hundreds of years of force inflicted fear. The fear that the African Diaspora people carry is rooted in discriminatory treatment and conditioning, convincing us of being "less than." Much of this fear created from bigotry has manifested itself in the form of an intergenerational curse passed down from slavery through the present day. A poverty-stricken mindset and lack of self-worth resonates into a second manifestation of slavery that many of us just can't seem to get past. Researcher, Dr. Molefi Kete Asante, developed the theory of Afrocentricity, which is a "paradigm based on the idea that African people should re-assert a sense of agency in order to achieve sanity," sanity being a way to eradicate ourselves from ill thoughts and fear of our own capabilities.

This is not to say that people of any ethnic group, economic status, and religion don't have fears that prevent them from moving forward in their lives—because all people at times wrap themselves in a state of worthlessness. Content or not with their life's plight, we cannot just accept that things are going to be the way they are instead of working toward a more abundant life. We all desire a life of happiness, wealth, and good health, surrounded by people who uplift us and who we can uplift. According to *Psychology Today*, "fear is often the base emotion on which anger [upset] floats." This book is for everyone who harbors fear that keeps them floating or wading in a pool of "I don't have what it takes." That *was* me! Every now and then, fear still tries to creep back up with splashes of worry and anxiety. Like in the song, "Wipe Me Down," by Lil Boosie; I say a prayer and just wipe the negativity and self-doubt away then step into my renewed faith.

I titled this introduction "*A* definition of fear" instead of "*The* definition of fear," because this book is meant to be a guide to help you understand the debilitating emotions you might have running rampant inside your mind and body. Its purpose is not to define who you are as a person or to generalize everyone's experience of fear. I will be sharing *my* journey and *my* victory, which I hope will be useful. But I want YOU to you find YOUR own path to victory.

When I was young, I hated my name—Tameka Nicole. It was one of the most popular names in the African American community at that time, coming in close behind Sarah in the White community. LOL! There was even a girl on the next street over who was also named Tamika Nicole! I knew I was not like everyone else on my block, so I didn't want the same name as everyone else. Also, I thought Tameka was a ghetto name which made me fear that because of my name; I would be judged by those outside my community. On my journey in learning more about myself, I studied the meaning of my name.

Tameka – Is Japanese in origin and is pronounced Tomiko, which means people

Nicole – Is Greek in origin and means victorious one!

That sums it up right there! I love people and through touching others' lives I have become victorious! Funny…Japanese food has always been my favorite maybe that's just a coincidence or maybe I was Japanese in another life. The name my mother and grandmother gave me, has now metamorphosed into a deep level of self-pride.

MY PERSONAL STORY

This book is portions, snippets, or as some say nuggets, of my life's experiences where fear got the best of me and how I overcame the hurt and loss which was a direct or indirect result of my own self-inflicted hallucinations of fear. I was born in the inner city of Cleveland, Ohio in 1976; ten years after the Hough riots which happened as a result of the poverty and racism felt in the African American communities in the late 1960. The riots contributed to economic decline in the area that lasted at least five decades. Recently, within the last decade and a half, city officials have made a point to revitalize the neighbor and try to attract wealthy upper-middle-class and upper-class people to the area. The Hough area is an extension of the Cleveland Clinic complex, which is currently ranked #2 in the Best Hospitals Honor Roll. Thus, having such a well-visited hospital in the vicinity of an economically depressed neighborhood is another reason the city has fought to improve the area.

I grew up in the Glenville area which is much like the Hough neighborhood. In 1968, just a few years after the Hough riots, the Glenville neighborhood attracted national news because of a shootout between Black Nationalists and the police. This shootout caused another riot in Cleveland, destroying over $2 million in property. As a result, the neighborhood remains one of the poorest sections of Cleveland. When I was born, Cleveland had been one of the main hubs for various forms of manufacturing because of the direct access to Lake Erie. Boats going in and out carried steel, apparel and other materials. This economic system would soon come to a halt with the loss of manufacturing primacy to overseas companies, causing another wave of poverty in the community.

I grew up in an apartment my entire life. (I didn't learn how to cut grass until I was almost 30 years old!) My mother was blessed enough to find a low-income townhouse that was NOT located in the projects. These types of apartments were few and far between, so my family was fortunate. I can only imagine how different my childhood would have been if I had to face not only our own poverty but mass poverty all around.

In my neighborhood there were some working-class people who owned their homes, unlike the federally subsidized housing projects that stretched up to 4 or 5 blocks wide and were often clustered next to other neighboring housing projects. This combination made for an intensely dangerous way of life filled with drugs, prostitution, burglary, and other crimes. This is not to say that my neighborhood was free from these poverty signifiers, but it was less pervasive and prolific.

My mother and father were 16 years of age when I was born. My brother came when they were 17, and then my sister was born while they were 21. My mom and dad split soon after my sister was born, and my dad became an inconsistent, unreliable part of our lives. He suffered from alcoholism in his 20s and 30s, and then when he began dabbling in crack cocaine my mother told him that he was not allowed to see us anymore. As my dad ran the streets, he kept slipping deeper into the proverbial rabbit hole, which led him to be sentenced to prison for 15 years on a felony charge.

Fighting was a way of life in the inner city. If you showed any level of fear, you would get pounced on. I grew up having to fight, sometimes self-provoked and many other times as a result of bullies running up on me. I often fought for my brother and sister; since I was the oldest, I carried the weight of protecting my siblings. Many times, I was victorious and others not so much. When I was about 12 years old, I remember a fight that my brother got into with a big hefty boy around the block. My brother came home crying and so I stomped my little self around the block and confronted this boy about my brother. "You wanna fight, well fight me." Now at the time I did not realize that at about 12 or 13 years of age is when boys begin to outgrow girls. This is when they begin to come into their young, initial stages of manhood. Previously, I would crush the boys that stepped to me or my brother. But this time was different. I was talking smack in this boy's face, and I hit him. This big hefty boy jumped his butt off the ground and gave me a Bruce Lee karate kick to my stomach, which sent me staggering back and almost falling to the ground. Later that day, I went home and told my brother, who was just a year younger than I, that he had to fight his own battles from now on.

As we got older, my fighting slowed down, and my brother and sister's fighting revved up. I think that was because I became more and more serious about getting educated so I could get the hell out of the 'hood. My sister and brother were unfortunately not as focused, and I came to learn that no matter how much I tried to help them get on the education pathway, I had to let go and allow them to find their own way. This was one of the hardest things I had to do. I knew that I was blessed with a special kind of tenacity that my siblings were still trying to develop. I was in constant fear that they would also fall down the rabbit hole. Thank the Lord, they did not.

I say all of this to say, I grew up in constant fear. Fear of the inner-city streets and always having to be on guard. I also had a fear that I was not going to be smart enough to get a job that would allow me to pull myself out of the quicksand of poverty. I began to seek mentors in school, church, and through the Upward Bound program (a federally funded college readiness program for first-generation and impoverished students). This is what differentiated me from my siblings and my friends who seemed to be caught and stagnant in a mindset of perpetual poverty. I shared my home life situations, my fears, and my dreams with my mentors, and they helped me see the world in a different light.

My Sunday school teacher Ms. Carol helped to save my life. As did my art teacher Ms. Levy and my industrial arts teacher Mr. Cleary who taught me everything I know about crafting leather. They showed me a life other than what was happening on my block. I began to become inquisitive about the world outside of 105th and St. Clair—outside of Cleveland. My desperate desire to leave my poverty-stricken neighborhood relinquished me of any fear I had about going to college and getting a job.

I got my high school diploma and got the hell out of dodge and have not looked back since. I promised myself that I would get as much knowledge and experience as I could and come back to teach and inspire others to do better. After graduating from college with a Bachelor of Arts degree in Fashion Design, I went to work as a designer for several large companies as well as a few smaller ones. After working for several years in the fashion industry, I decided to go back to school and get a Master of Arts degree in Apparel and Textile Design. Once I completed my M.A. I got back into the fashion industry and discovered my design niche: Technical Design. Techs are the engineers of the clothing we wear every day. Techs can detail a garment down to the number of stitches needed to keep it together, and I'm a damn good tech!

After meeting my husband, I left the fashion industry and went back to school for my Ph.D. While I was in working toward my degree, I started teaching part-time at the Fashion School at Kent State University. I fought my way through the ranks at Kent State and became the university's first African American professor of fashion in 2012 (and currently as I write this, I still am the only African American fashion professor). The next phase of my life is my entrepreneurial journey, and here is where you, my reader, comes into my life.

My fears have been elevated to my SUPERPOWERS. Soaring leaps and bounds over all others in my field, I am only the receiver and the transformer of the gifts God gave me. Now that's the short and skinny. Ready to learn how I did it???

THE SUPERPOWER DISCLAIMER

Before you embark on this journey, I want you to ask yourself, "Why? Why am I doing this?" "What? What do I expect to get out of the strategies from this book?" "How? How can I implement some or all of these strategies into my life?" Are you ready to receive? If not, what would it take for you get ready? No one can do it for you. You must make up your mind that you are ready to enhance your life, you have to make it up in your mind that you were ready to show who you know your best self to be!

"A principle (external) is only as good as the spirit/person (internal) that it comes into contact with. When a principle encounters someone who has not developed a proper environment that will allow it to grow, nothing really happens,"

-R. J. Hodges.

I am ready to share my journey of courage and love. I sure hope you are ready to receive it. If you have a challenging time with allowing the strategies to resonate with you, please take as long as you need to regroup; and then come back. I know there is something in this book that will help ignite your superpowers!

My love always,

Dr. Tameka N. Ellington
(A First Generation Revolutionary)

CHAPTER 1

FEAR OF YOUR VOICE

I begin with this type of fear because in order for me to write this book, I had to own my fear, interrogate it, break it down and then use it as fuel. I grew up in a household of a strong single mother who had strict rules in order to keep my brother, sister and I on the straight and narrow. My mother was raised to believe, and she raised us to believe, that children should be seen and not heard. This was a coping mechanism that many African Americans took as a means of survival. There was a time in history where our voice was not recognized as a valid human voice. African Americans were taught to believe that we were not human; therefore, how could we possibly have a voice or opinion about the world. This principle lasted for many decades in order to keep a community of people safe from violent bigotry. This manifested itself into the method of how African Americans raise their children in an attempt to keep them safe. I'm sure you all are familiar with the phrase "My way or the highway!"

For those that don't know, this phrase is what parents tell their children when they feel their children are being disobedient or disrespectful. This is understandable, from a respect standpoint. I'm a parent, so I know how important it is for children to respect their parents, elders, and others. However, this phrase "my way or the highway" is stifling to the future voice of a person Growing up I was taught that my opinion didn't matter in my household. And so, for the most part, when it came to discussing how I felt about various matters, I usually kept quiet. Now, as a mother of two young boys and a young man, although I am strict when it comes to my children respecting me and other adults, I also believe that it is extremely important for them to be able to talk to me and give me their opinion about the runnings of our household or their thoughts about the world.

And in some ways this principle manifested in other ways in my life, including in my marriage. I had to work on my communication (or lack thereof). And I'm still working on it....

Unfortunately, not being allowed to express myself as a child made me extremely afraid to voice my opinions and to speak up for myself as an adult. From an early age, I've always considered myself a leader. But I was what I referred to as a silent leader. In junior high school (what we also referred to as intermediate school) I was the captain of our drill team. My team looked to me for guidance and leadership. I made sure our team was organized, and I helped develop many of the routines. However, I didn't have a big enough voice to call the commands during our performances. My co-captains always called the commands. I was too fearful to speak in a commandingly strong voice for my team. Being afraid of my voice limited the type of experience I had and the type of influence I could have had over my team. I could never have dreamed then of being the type of captain that I know I am capable of being now. In my 8th grade year, with me serving as captain, the team won 1st place at the Cleveland Public Schools drill team competition. It was indeed a result of my managerial and people skills; however, I can't take credit for the big voice that helped to reel in our win.

In high school I was the vice president of our student council. I knew I had the capabilities to be president, but I just didn't have the confidence to get up in front of my entire student body and give a speech. Just the thought of that made me want to throw up! This one instance kept me from my full potential. I was too afraid of being embarrassed for saying the wrong thing or mispronouncing a word in front of everybody. I didn't feel like I had a strong enough voice and what I had to say could not possibly be important enough for the entire student body to pay attention.

A fear of your voice—written or verbal—translates into how you truly feel about yourself as a person. Is your perspective valuable to the world? Yes, it is! No matter where you come from, how you were raised, or your family situation—YOUR voice matters!

During an interview on the podcast hosted by Brother Bedford, *Conversations with Black Millionaire Entrepreneurs*, entrepreneur and former college professor, Dr. Venus Opal Reese discussed growing up on the impoverished streets of Boston, Massachusetts. Under unfortunate circumstances she found herself homeless as a teenager. The alleyways and street corners became her home. She passionately spoke about her conditions and revealed that one day she found herself sitting in the corner alley, drunk and reeking of piss. She pleaded to God to help her. After that moment, her life began to change. God sent her a dedicated mentor and friend who helped to develop her sense of self-worth, and she began to put her new reimagined self into action. The fears she felt about being accepted in the world because of her circumstances soon faded away. Today she is one of the most prolific speakers motivating Black women to be their best selves.

A fear of your voice perpetuates low levels of self-esteem and self-efficacy. Dr. Morris Rosenberg, a pioneer in the theory of self-esteem, discusses that self-esteem is an overall general positive or negative feeling toward ourselves—our self-worth These feelings are often a direct result of external phenomena in our world, such as discrimination, a tragic accident that has left us dismembered, an exhilarating race where we came in first place, or being validated at work by our colleagues with an award. So of course, it works for the good and the bad. Self-esteem also comes from our perceptions of others' attitudes towards us. Do I feel capable amongst my peers?? Am I likeable?

During my first experiences in the classroom, I was terrified that my students would hate me, and that they would know that I really didn't know what the hell I was doing. I found myself "faking it until I made it"! I still remember it like yesterday, as I prepared to walk into my first ever class—a sophomore-level drawing class at Michigan State University—I had the overwhelming feeling of nausea. I had never felt my stomach in knots like this before. As I stepped into the classroom in my cute grey pleated skirt (at least I looked like I was ready—if those kids only knew how I felt on the inside) I slunk to the front of the class and stumbled with my supplies. My first words came out scratchy and jagged. As I began talking with the students and we all introduced ourselves, my nerves eased up a bit; but it would take years of me being in front of a classroom before I felt confident and knowledgeable enough to be their professor. Part of my insecurity stemmed from the fact that my classroom demographic was 95 percent young White women, and most of them had never had an African American teacher. So yes, I was intimidated. My poverty-stricken upbringing would creep back into my mind, and I would tell myself I wasn't smart enough to teach these young women. I had a real self-efficacy problem.

SELF-EFFICACY AND YOUR VOICE

Self-efficacy is a subcategory or, scientifically speaking, a domain-specific type of self-esteem. This domain is exclusive to our attitudes and behaviors toward what we feel we are capable of doing. According to Albert Bandura, acclaimed psychologist and professor, "Expectations of personal efficacy are derived from four principle sources of information: performance accomplishments, vicarious experience, verbal persuasion, and physiological states." Now let's break this down.

Performance accomplishments: things you do well and are rewarded for. Accomplishments makes us feel great and, in some instances, invincible. This principle has the ability to drive us into continued success of tasks or jobs that we know we are good at. The tasks or jobs may be challenging or not; however, there is a comfort level that comes with knowing what we can accomplish well.

Vicarious experiences: those experiences we have by observing others. We often think to ourselves, "If they can do it, I know I can do it!" We get excited when we see tasks or jobs done well by others. Vicarious experiences can work on our behalf or work against us. Having a fearful mindset will make you doubt yourself and take the learned experiences that you had and turn them against you.

Verbal persuasion: what we verbally speak about our capabilities or how others verbally encourage us or tear us down. Do you ever talk yourself out of doing things because of fear? If you do, here is where that fear lives. Do you need others to pump you up to take a risk? We all do at some time in our lives. We are human and we want to know that we have support from family, friends and colleagues.

Physiological: the way in which our body reacts to our experiences. This part of us affects our heart rate (among other physical reactions!) due to the release of adrenaline in response to the fight or flight response. Also, attitudes effect behaviors. Thus, your mental attitude is critical!!

While in my doctoral program, I took a course taught by my one of my mentors, Dr. Joanne Dowdy, called Black Women in Literacy. My classmates and I had been tossing around ideas about topics for our dissertation, and I was excited that I had finally confirmed my topic. Or at least I *thought* I had. Since my background was in Fashion, and I was getting my Ph.D. in Education, the dilemma became how to tie those two fields together? Through months of deliberation in this class and several others, I had decided to study African American high school girls and their educational attainment. I wanted to find out if their level of self-esteem and the way they dressed had an effect on their schooling.

Dr. Dowdy asked us to come back to class the following week with an abstract (short summary) about the premise of our dissertation topic. Since I had nailed down my topic, I was pumped and excited about delivering my paper to my class. So, when it became my turn, I stood up and read my abstract with enthusiastic pride! After I finished, I started to sit down and just before my rear-end completely touched the seat, my classmate (one of the only other African American Ph.D. students I met during my time in school) said, "Have you ever thought of researching the *self-efficacy* of African American girls in comparison with their self-esteem? I have heard that their self-efficacy is quite different than their self-esteem." I immediately cut my eyes at her. My pride was making it difficult to recognize the value of her suggestion, so I responded gruffly with, "Um, no I haven't. I'll have to look into that." Knowing damn well I didn't even know what self-efficacy was. After class I went home and started researching the term and fishing through academic articles to learn all I could about African American girls and their self-efficacy. My classmate was right—with this new added variable, my research would be much stronger. My dissertation title became "Dress and Self-efficacy as they Relate to the Academic Achievement and Future Goals of African American High School Girls."

During my research, I started evaluating the self-esteem versus the self-efficacy of African American girls and their White counterparts. Interestingly, I learned that African American girls have very high self-esteem while White girls had lower self-esteem. African American girls grew up with more personal, "love yourself"-type affirmations at home than most White girls had. On the flip side, White girls had a higher self-efficacy because they received more motivational, "you can do it" affirmations at home than African American girls had. Also, White girls BELIEVED the affirmations! This is the key! Both girls had faced sexist societal gender roles; however, White girls were not faced with the same racial discrimination African American girls dealt with. A prime example of intersectionality.

Intersectionality theory was introduced by civil right activist, critical race and feminist scholar Kimberlé Crenshaw. This theory was developed as an analytical strategy to examine the discriminatory crossovers in social inequality. History has shown that African Americans as a whole are STILL working to pull themselves out of the economic and educational gap. African Americans in many cases, still do not possess the mental attitude necessary to have a fearless persona regarding sharing their voice with the world. For hundreds of years African Americans AND women were told that their voices did not matter. The intersectionality of being African American and being a woman created double doses of the snuffing-out of their opinions, thoughts, and their overall contributions to society. No wonder African American women have to work harder at gaining adequate self-efficacy and mental attitude levels.

Dennis Kimbro, author and entrepreneur discusses that a change in mental attitude from negative to positive perspectives of oneself is a REMOVAL of emotions stemming from fear by means of faith and prayer. The POWER of faith and prayer can help us overcome the debilitating fear that is connected to our low self-efficacy. Often times when we fear our voice doesn't matter, conformity becomes the logical and best answer. When we conform, we blend in; we don't draw attention to ourselves or allow others to see how our unique superpowers. When we conform, it is a grave tragedy because no one gets to experience OUR peak perfection. And what I mean by perfection is someone being in their ultimate self, being exactly who they are meant to be. When you step into your greatness, conformity is not an option. The fear that you had regarding whether you will be accepted by others is no longer a concern. What a FREEING thought!

When I think about this notion, often times it brings me back to my teenage years. All teenagers at one point or other want to fit in. Being different can cause strife in a teenager's life. When in all actuality, none of us are exactly like anyone else anyway. If we have to work extra hard to be "normal" or to "fit in," what does that say about us as a people? It says that we are tolerating the idea of snuffing out our voice. Fitting in is for the fearful—not those with grand SUPERPOWERS!

CHAPTER 2

FEAR OF PUBLIC SPEAKING

Oh, my goodness!! Public speaking was my enemy for MANY, MANY years. This is a different concept than fearing your voice. As we saw in the previous chapter, fear of your voice is more about feelings of worthiness and knowing that what you have to contribute to the world really does matter. This chapter is about the ability to get up in front of people and share your thoughts and expertise. Whether it is in a classroom setting, an interview, or on stage in front of 10,000 people, public speaking can cause anxiety and angst.

The term *glossophobia* means speech anxiety or fear of public speaking. The term glossophobia is derived from the Greek word *glōssa*, meaning tongue, and *phobos*, fear or dread. According to research done at the University of Tennessee Knoxville, it has been estimated that 75% of all people experience some form of speech anxiety. When I think about my first experiences with public speaking, and how much of a wreck I was, I just thank God that I've come as far as I have.

IN THE BEGINNING, THERE WAS THE GREAT ST, ST, STAMMER...

After finishing school, like all new college graduates, I began looking for a job and go through the interviewing process, which was grueling for me. Up until that point, I had never really had to do a formal interview. I worked since I was 12 years old, but mostly with my own little businesses. I did great work with my art and with braiding hair, so most of my clients came through word-of-mouth. Although I did eventually have a "real job" working the Cavs games at Cleveland's Gund Arena stadium during my senior year in high school, the interview was very low pressure. The manager of the hostess company was just looking for bodies to fill her positions, so I got through that interview with flying colors.

During my college years as an undergraduate I had a very similar situation regarding job placement. I still had my business braiding hair, and I worked as a peer mentor for the Cleveland Scholarship Program. This program was developed for Cleveland Public School students to gain monies towards college. The Cleveland Scholarship Program allowed you to earn money for making good grades; A's were worth $100 and B's were worth $50. I graduated within the 10th percentile of my in high school class, which meant I came out with over $4,000 in scholarship money. As a result of my high achievements, during the start of my sophomore year in college, I was invited by the Kent State University Cleveland Scholarship Program staff coordinator to be the peer mentor to the incoming students who were also awardees of the program. Again, this was a job I did not really have to interview for.

In August 1999 my undergraduate graduation rolls around, which meant it was time for me to begin looking for a job in the fashion industry. My classmates and I had all taken a course to help in the development of our resumes and cover letters, as well as with interviewing strategies via mock-interview practice. Our instructor set us up in a room with bright lights, a video camera and a small round table where we had to sit across from a fashion professional who had volunteered her time to do mock interviews with the students. It became time for my mock interview session and when I sat down at the table, my heart immediately started palpitating. I don't know if it was the bright lights or the fact that I knew my session was being recorded, but I straight BOMBED that interview! Years later I looked at the VHS tape, and it was disgraceful to see me shaking like a leaf and every other word that came out of my mouth was "um." By the grace of God, when my real interview for my first job in the fashion industry came up, I somehow got through it and was able to begin my new career as a designer. I don't know HOW that happened; it's all a blur at this point.

After working for few years in the fashion industry, one of my professors, Melanie Carrico, emailed me and asked if I would come and speak to her class of 100+ students about my experience transitioning from school into the industry. Of course, I said yes. I was honored to be asked. But then came the task of preparing my lecture and getting up in front of the students and presenting said lecture. With an outline of what I wanted to share scribbled in a little notepad, I got dressed in my best suit and heels, got in my car and drove to campus to meet the students, to give them some tips and strategies on securing their spot in the fashion industry. When I arrived I gave Melanie a hug, and I made my way to the front of the class. I walked up on stage and to the podium. When I got there and had the chance to look out at the audience for the first time at ALL the students, I just froze. I stammered my way through the ENTIRE presentation and instead of leaving the students with tips and strategies, I more or less left them with my stuttering and my "deer trapped in the headlights" impression. Man, it was just awful!

MY NEWFOUND CONFIDENCE AND GROWTH IN PUBLIC SPEAKING

Today, I can get up in front of a room and speak to anyone, but that came after years of practice with my students and invited speaking engagements. Every semester, I got better and better at presenting the lessons and even became better at interacting with my students on an individual basis. It all comes down to confidence and not having a fear of your voice! When you believe that you DO have a right to speak your mind and you DO believe that people will value what you have to say, your fear of public speaking will begin to vanish. My inner-city upbringing and society's discriminatory perceptions of being a poor, Black girl made me doubt my right to get up and share my knowledge and certainly evoked the *glassophobia* in me.

There are numerous advantages to becoming comfortable with public speaking. One of the most important is the self-improvement that comes along with speaking. It builds a confidence in you that you would have never known existed until you get up in from of a crowd of people. *Virtual Speech* lists 16 benefits to developing the ability to speak publicly:

1. Career advancement and building credibility
2. Boost confidence
3. Critical thinking; writing a speech requires a great deal of careful thought
4. Personal development
5. Improves communication skills
6. Make new social connections of people in a similar field as you
7. Personal satisfaction
8. Expand your professional network
9. Learn to persuade
10. Build leadership skills
11. Learn performance skills, become conscious of timing, learning how to shift through changes of volume, speech rate and tone

12. Develop your vocabulary and fluency
13. No fear of impromptu speaking
14. Learn how to put forward a well thought out argument
15. Helps you drive change, the more people you're able to speak to, the more change you can implement
16. Be a better listener, learning what message others need to hear

Public speaking experience goes a long way in that it develops in you the strength to do unbelievable things. For instance, the first time I spoke to one of my idols, networking guru and entrepreneur, Dr. George Fraser; I was terrified! I was connected with him through Dr. Kwa David Whitaker (a United States citizen who took on the amazing journey of becoming an African Chief), and when the time came to connect with Dr. Fraser, I had to muster up all the confidence I had and drop the celebrity gaga mode! Dr. Fraser and I arranged to speak on the phone, and after we exchanged a brief introduction of ourselves; he laid everything out flat, no fluff or sugar. "So, who are your targeting, and how are you reaching them?" he asked me. I had prepared this in my mind more in depth before our conversation, but the best response that I could get out was, "the youth and young professionals." Dr. Fraser's comeback was, "Well, you are not going to reach them with this book you're writing! Most young people are on social media! Dr. George Fraser told me that if I am going to reach this demographic, I *have* to beef up my social media platforms. My Facebook account was not going to be enough. Yes, I knew that... but as a 40 something supposedly-hip chic, it was hard to hear that dose of reality from a 70 something distinguished gentleman! I took his "real" advice and grew from it.

My passion is connecting with and inspiring young people—high school students, college students, young professionals, and others who are on their way to becoming a first-generation revolutionary. A first-generation revolutionary is someone who was the first in their family to go to college or a first-generation immigrant to a new country. These individuals have completed college and have a great career or started a successful business. Many times, people who are first generation, come from a low-income background or from middle- or higher-income families without a college-going tradition. The distinction of a revolutionary is one who has gained success and reaches back into their communities to uplift others who were just like them. My service goals to elevate high school students, college students, young professionals, and future first-generation revolutionaries, gives me a BIGGER reason to be on social media platforms. So, believe me, I'm ON it!!

MY FIRST LIFE CHANGING SPEECH

The first confirmation that I had given a life-changing speech came when I was invited to be the keynote speaker for the Kent State University Upward Bound high school graduating class of 2014. The title of my speech was, "Let's Make this Simple: Are You an Eagle or Turkey?" The message gave me the opportunity to give deep review of the phrase How can you fly like an eagle, if you are surrounded by turkeys? During my lecture I showed a beautiful slide presentation on a black background filled with witty photos including images of turkeys and eagles facing off and the red circular 'no' symbol looming over a turkey in representation of the need for a self-reflecting look at the suspected turkeys in the audience. I told stories about my life on St. Clair Avenue in Cleveland and how I was constantly surrounded by folks with no drive and who couldn't understand *why* I had drive—a.k.a., the turkeys. I discussed what success looked like for me at that time and what success could look like for the new graduates. In the last portion of my speech, I had a photo of a plain turkey sandwich with the heading "How to handle the turkeys." My final words were:

"So when a jive turkey tells you to your face or behind your back (because you know, they do that kind of thing all the time) that you can't make it... How do you handle that jive turkey? How can you fly like an eagle when you are surrounded by turkeys? You pick yourself up, shake yourself off, and leave those turkeys right where they are—on the ground! You show those turkeys who you belong to. You show them you are a child of God and you will not be stifled! You roast those turkeys up, slice them and dice them, and you have them for lunch!!

After my presentation, I received a standing ovation. Numerous people came up to me thanking me for the inspiring words and congratulating me for the success that I'd been able to accomplish. A friend of mine, Dr. Keith

Wisdom, approached me after and ecstatically declared, "You need to take that show on the road!" I didn't quite understand what he meant at that time, but now I totally get it!

I've been able to accomplish so many things in my life, and I look forward to accomplishing more! My main goal is to bring my community along with me in a bigger way than I could have ever imaged. So yeah, I have a whole lot to say and I have a whole lot to share, and I have had to develop the public speaking skills that can allow me to do just that.

Today, before a speaking event, I get as prepared as I can. Rehearsing my speech, making sure I have a great outfit to wear, my hair and makeup done just right, I get enough sleep the day before, and I say a prayer right before going on stage: "Lord, give me the words to say. You have made ME the expert on this topic. You have blessed ME with this knowledge and wisdom, and it would be a sin not to share it!" I repeat that a few times and I can feel my confidence building. My back begins to straighten, so that my posture is at attention, and then I march out onto the stage as if I own it. I kill the speech and say a thanks of gratitude to God for getting me through it.

I have to confess I've been daydreaming about a certain speaking engagement for some time, and now—I'm putting it out into the Universe! One of my next speaking engagements WILL BE at the graduation ceremony for my alma mater, Glenville High School. I want to connect with the graduating Tarblooders by telling them my story of how I was once in their seats, how I started off stammering over my words, to several years later becoming an Associate Dean and a newly born Entrepreneur!

GOD IS SO GOOD!! He can take the meager and transform it into a masterpiece! Thanks to my membership with *Toastmasters International*, I will continue to build and perfect my speaking abilities. I've never been one for mediocrity: I'm a damn good designer, I'm an even better educator, and now I'm striving toward being a dynamite speaker! After years of practice with public speaking, I still get butterflies, but this is no longer a result of my fearfulness. These butterflies are my "get pumped" vibes. They are my SUPERPOWERS!

CHAPTER 3

FEAR OF RELATIONSHIPS

When I talk about relationships, I'm not just talking about the romantic kind. The relationships that we have with our parents, with our siblings, and with our friends can be manipulated by fear. Relationships are so difficult—I wish God would've made them easier! Good relationships take time and effort. Good relationships take understanding and appreciation and respect from the people involved. It doesn't matter if you're in a romantic relationship or a friendship, the elements of understanding and respect are very important and are the foundation of any relationship. When we feel rejected by others with whom we are attempting to have a relationship, we become fearful that we are not lovable.

UNLOVABLE—JUST FOR BEING YOU

Research suggests that people who have a low self-esteem are chronically motivated to protect themselves from *expected* rejection. Having a low self-esteem, especially regarding relationships, puts us at risk of feeling unlovable. We have all been there at one time in our lives, whether self-inflected or brought on from being rejected by someone else. Many times, when someone doesn't show love to you, it has absolutely nothing to do with who you as a person. Maybe something is holding them back, maybe they don't know how to love because they were never previous shown true love. When you desperately want someone to love you, that becomes a hard pill to swallow and a concept that you can barely wrap your brain around.

We almost all the time put the onus back on ourselves: "Hmm, something must be wrong with *me*," and we ask ourselves, "What did I ever do to this person for them not to love me?" It's never a simple solution but taking yourself out of the equation and looking at the entire situation really helps. It won't always make you feel better, but it will give you a better perspective on what is really happening, and hopefully get you to stop blaming yourself.

Feeling unlovable can become coupled with being "successful"—be it in your career, love life, or some other aspect of your life. When you grow up in an environment where you rarely see people striving to be better, becoming "successful" automatically makes you an outlier. It truly takes a strong-willed, positive attitude not to fall into this self-hatred trap. Because we all want to be loved and appreciated, we will at times sacrifice our own happiness or what we know to be our true selves just to be loved. One of those ways is by not fully celebrating your achievements in life. As a first-generation revolutionary, I know this all too well. For me, growing up in a habitually unwed, impoverished environment, then becoming one of the only people from that environment who was educated, married, and who had acquired a bit of financial freedom made for a lonely existence. People started to tell me that they didn't know how to relate to me, like I was suddenly a different person or something.

In relationships when we downplay our successes to make others feel comfortable, this is another form of conformity. Sometimes people have a hard time with our successes, and in romantic, familial, *and* platonic relationships we strive to make the other people comfortable. So… we don't talk about the awards and/or promotions that we may have gotten at work or the new accounts we have acquired in our business. Or we don't share the great news we just received that we've been waiting months to hear. All of this secrecy, which ends up stifling our joy, is a direct result of our fear of being alone. (For REAL!) If you have acquired a bit of success in your life, you may have been or will be told that you are "bragging" or that "you think you're better than the next person." Again, take yourself out of the equation: look at things on a grander scale and try not to take offense from the insecure comments made by others!

I'm guilty of deemphasizing my successes with people who I should have been able to talk to about them. On this journey, I had to realize that it is ok not to tell EVERYONE about the successes you have in your life. The issue becomes when you change up the story about your successes just so that you won't seem to be braggadocious. I think back to a time in my life when I had this very problem with my mother. Much of what I was doing in my life in regard to school, getting rewards or accolades, or just the day-to-day experiences I was having, I would not share or I would reduce my accomplishments so that it didn't seem as though I was boasting. I remember hearing people in my family say, "you think you're better than (such and such)." When in all actuality, I was just being who I am and who God sent me here to be. The bottom line is if people have a tough time accepting your shine, that's their problem not yours.

QUALMS IN MY RELATIONSHIP WITH MY MOTHER

My mother in particular had many things to say about my success, and much of what she said was negative. At one point she didn't even want to be left in a room with me by herself for fear she wouldn't know how to have a conversation with me. Whenever I asked her to lunch, she *always* invited my sister. I absolute love spending time with my sister, but I would have liked to have had some alone time with my mother. Just recently was the first time I ever spent time with my mom alone. My sister and my mom spend much more time together because they live closer in proximity, so they would do little things just the two of them almost every other weekend. Whenever I would ask my mother to hang out with me for lunch or some other activity, she would always ask my sister to come, "Well, okay but let me see if your sister can come too," as if she didn't feel comfortable hanging with me without my sister.

The worst argument that my mother and I had ever gotten into was on Mother's Day 2013. And you have to understand, I never argued with her; she was always arguing with me. I am a true believer that you must respect your elders, even if sometimes they're not doing the right things. After a few years of trying, I had finally got my mom to agree to lunch just she and I. During the planning, I explained to her that I would have to take her the weekend *before* Mother's Day because my cousin was graduating from college on Mother's Day, and I wanted to be there to support him. He was the first and still the only male in our family to graduate with a four-year college degree. There was no way I was missing that!! Our lunch weekend came, and my mother bailed on me! She told me that her boyfriend wanted to take her out that weekend, and she had to cancel our date. So, even though I agreed, in the back of my mind I was thinking to myself, "She really can't just sit at a table with me and have a conversation." I was pissed and hurt.

The day of my cousin's graduation came. To put things into perspective, this particular cousin was the step-son of my blood cousin. Therefore, my cousin was not "blood," but he was family to me, and I was extremely proud that he was graduating from college, because until then I was 1 of 2 people in my family to get a college degree. His graduation was out of town, and I asked my mom to babysit my kids so that I can attend, while my husband was at work. As I mentioned, my cousin's graduation was scheduled on Mother's Day at 1:00 in the afternoon. After the 3-hour drive and roaming around the campus until I found the building where the graduation was going to be held, the time was approximately 11:30 am. Before I found my seat at the ceremony, I decided to call my mom and wish her a Happy Mother's Day.

I was definitely not prepared for her reaction! She flipped out on me for not calling and wishing her a Happy Mother's Day *earlier* in the morning. As soon as I got on the phone, she began screaming at me. She was telling me that I didn't care about her because I went to the graduation of a cousin who wasn't even "blood," instead of spending the day with her. Remember, because I knew that I was going to be at the graduation, I had invited my mom out to lunch the week BEFORE, and she cancelled on me.

So here I am at my cousin's graduation huddled up in a corner in the hallway trying to have this frustratingly agitating call with my mom who was on the other end of the phone cursing me out. As I tried to explain my position in this whole situation, she hits me with, "You don't love me. The only daughter of mine that loves me is your sister. Since you don't care nothing about me, you are no longer my daughter!" As you might imagine, otherwise, I would have been hurt, but after years of this same type of badgering, I was boiling mad. The blood rushing to my head was about to make my face explode. I wasn't going to cry, because at this point, I was done crying because of the things that she said to me or did to me. I was PISSED!

Throughout my life, I've done nothing but respect my mom, even when she wasn't doing right by me or my siblings. I called my husband immediately and asked him to go and pick our kids up from my mom. And I told him I was done with her. I was certain that I was not going to ever speak to her again unless she apologized to me, which she's never done in her whole life, so I had to be ready to accept the fact that I might not talk to my mom ever again.

When the holidays came around, I avoided going to any place I knew she was going to be. It bothered my brother so much that he called me one day almost in tears about that fact that my mother and I hadn't spoken to each other in almost a year. He tried to rationalize with me that I needed to call her, but I was sticking to my guns: "I have done nothing wrong; she was the one who disrespected me and said nasty things to me. Therefore, I was not going to speak to her unless she was ready to apologize." My brother and I hung up the phone, me in my frustration and him in his despair. A few days later he calls me, and says, "Mommy is ready to apologize."

On a chilly spring day in March or April, I can't remember exactly, I try to push negativity out of my mind and not give it much real estate to be harped on. I'm still working on that! I went to my mother's apartment, which was near a park with walking trails and playground equipment. She and I decided to go across the street to the park and talk while we walked the trail. As we walked, we shared our feelings about our relationship and cried along the way. And what it all came down to was that my mother was afraid that I thought she wasn't good enough to be my mother. She was afraid that she was unlovable and that I was going to *eventually* reject her as my mother. She said, "Well, you went to school and got all those degrees now. You're so smart and you're doing so many things with your life. I just didn't think I was good enough to be your mom." WOW! So much hurt over so many years could have been wiped away if I had known that sooner.

This situation is a perfect example of what Lisa Nichols refers to as **FEAR** being the effects of **F**alse **E**vidence **A**ppearing **R**eal. My mother sacrificed so much to make sure that we had the best life she could offer. I understand now that my mother's treatment wasn't because she didn't love me; it was because she was afraid for our relationship. She had a false idea of who I was because of her low self-esteem and therefore, she wanted to reject me before I had the opportunity to reject her. Through all the heartache, I was ready to totally give up my relationship with my mother because I was afraid that she was going to keep hurting me.

Now I know that the strife I had with my mother was a direct result of her fear that I would see her as a "less-than" or inadequate mother after I earned my PhD, even though I had *never* said anything of that nature to her or to anyone else. Thank God she and I both had a revelation! We now have a better relationship than we've ever had. I use our past as my SUPERPOWER—my fuel and strength for what our relationship CAN become. Today our relationship is a work in progress. I can call her for anything, and she will call me for anything, a stark difference from how things were in the past. Taking care of my mother is my main goal. If I have anything to do with it, she will live comfortably in her retirement.

THE WOES OF FINDING AND KEEPING FRIENDSHIPS

Once I became a professional, finding other professional African American friends became difficult. Most times, white collar African Americans are surrounded by White people all day long. I have wonderful friends of all races, but there is nothing like having a friend that you don't have to explain cultural innuendos to, they just get your struggle. I'm sure my Korean friends love me, but they really love having other Korean friends around—someone who knows the language and the culture. And in some cases, an African American person may be the only African American in their department or at their place of employment, period. It's very isolating!

I had long since let go of many of the toxic people who were stuck, stagnating and going nowhere with their lives. Unfortunately, many of these people are African American. As the mother of 2 small boys, my goal was to find other African American moms with small kids. After some time,

NOT finding African American friends that had a similar family structure was taxing on me. That struggle was real! I kept running into these moms who had kids the same age as mine, but then the moms were in their late 20s or they were single! By this time, I was over 35 years old, married, and established. I could not even image letting a new person into my life who was that young! I had met a successful African American woman who was the mother of a small child. I thought she would fit the bill; but she ended up being an insecure, crazy woman—the type who doesn't like constructive criticism and cannot be happy for her friends and their successes. Especially, if those successes outshined hers. Ain't nobody got time for that ridiculousness, so as easy as I picked her up, I put her down.

To my husband's disapproval, I joined Jack and Jill of America, Inc. Jack and Jill is an organization that was started in the 1930s as a way for professional African American families to get their children together for play dates and outings. This was so important because African Americans were prohibited from going to many public family spaces, such as public parks and pools. Jack and Jill made a way for African American families to stay connected. I love the premise of what the organization stands for and that's why I joined. After spending 2 years of my family's time in the group, I decided that it was not for me and my family. It was being run similar to a sorority, and I had not signed up for that. Neither my husband or I belonged to a fraternity or sorority, and it became apparent that this organization was not a great fit for us. Once again, I was on the hunt to find friends.

More and more African American women got hired at Kent State University. I started getting to know those women, and my friendship pool began to swell. Individually, I had a relationship with many of them, and we would go out to lunch and hang out. In 2016 my husband and I started on the journey of building a new house. We moved in by Fall 2017, and we hosted a housewarming party during the summer of. 2018. I thought that this party would be the perfect time to get ALL my women friends from Kent State together! My fear of not finding friends became my SUPERPOWER to have the guts to put all of these highly educated African American women together in the same room.

In a personal, and many times a professional environment, rarely is there ever more than 1-2 African American women who hold a doctorate degree in the same space. Only 5-6% of African Americans (men and women) get a Master's degree, and about 1% obtain a PhD. My housewarming party turned into an amazing display of Black Girl Magic!! I finally felt that I had been able to surround myself with a totality of friendships of likeminded women. What's wonderful is that all of the women are supportive of one another! We can laugh together, cry together, and pray together. No one feels left out or like their opinion doesn't matter.

My fear of not finding friends had come to a pause. Through my growth and personal development, my perspective on the world has changed so much that it might be easier now to move through life with fewer relationships if I had to. I feel more whole and full than I ever have in my life, but I'm still a work in progress!! Although of course I try to maintain my great friendships, I know that everything will be ok, as long as I'm on the journey to lifelong betterment. That way, I can bring people (like my readers!) with me.

CHAPTER 4

FEAR OF
SOCIETAL INEQUALITY

This chapter is meant to be a support for the underrepresented people reading this book. If you are not affiliated with underrepresented populations and you are reading this, it's still important for you to carefully read so that you can get a better understanding of how hundreds of years of subordination affects and debilitates a whole race of people. Robert Merton's 1948 book *Self-fulfilling Prophecy* helps to put in perspective the reason African Americans as a community continue to be stagnant. A self-fulfilling prophecy "is in the beginning, a false definition of a situation evoking a new behavior which makes the original false concept come true. This specious validity of the self-fulfilling prophecy perpetuates a reign of error. For the prophet will cite the actual course of events as proof that he was right from the very beginning."

MY FIRST EXPEREINCE WITH RACISM

I remember the first time I really felt racism directed toward me. I was a freshman in undergraduate at Kent State University. My resident assistant (RA) gave some paint to each of the residents on our floor so that we could decorate the wall in front of our door. I was on the second floor in Wright Hall, a tall, nine-story building. My room was directly across from the elevator. Our RA asked us to paint something that "reflects who we are." I painted a 6-foot image of Africa in red, black, and green, the colors of the Afro-American flag. I painted a beautiful image of Queen Nefertiti and Pharoh Tutankhamun. I painted on the phrase, "Africa, the home of Kings and Queens." I just can imagine myself stepping back and looking at my finished piece, feeling quite proud. Every day when I would leave out of my room to get ready to go to class I would see my artwork and be reminded of my royal blood and my divine connection to all mankind. I know was a freshman so I probably wasn't thinking that deep, but I was sure as hell proud to be African American.

When I first came to Kent State University it was a major culture shock for me. Growing up in the inner-city, the only people I saw were people who looked like me. Black and beautiful, but poor. Coming to a predominately White school made me feel isolated; in my classes often times I would be the only person of color. I had never before seen that many White people, I wondered where the hell did all of them come from. On my dorm floor, I met my very first White friend, Sarah. She was a spunky brunette girl from Chicago. She had a fun spirit, and I loved hanging out with her. She ended up leaving Kent State University and transferring to another school. She and I kept in touch for a few years after but since then, I lost touch with her. I still think about her every now and again.

One day I was coming out of my dorm room to go to class, and I passed by my African painting. Someone had spit over the entire wall—I'm talking about that nasty type of hawking phlegm spit!! I was devastated! I couldn't believe that people could be so mean. I went and told my RA, and she had someone come and clean the wall for me. At that very moment, I knew that racism and discrimination were real. I never before felt it because I never before encountered White people in that way.

There were a few White people that went to my high school, but they were all poor inner-city kids just like me. They were outnumbered by hundreds of African American kids, so there were never any issues. Plus, the White students couldn't put up much of a fuss after school because they were bussed over to the eastside of Cleveland with the school-integration policy that started in the 1980s. Cleveland is one of the most segregated cities in all of the United States. The East-siders and the West-siders: never shall the twain meet. Hence, another reason why I had never seen a mass number of White people like I witnessed when arriving on the Kent State University campus.

MANUIPLATION OF THE BLACK MIND

For years African Americans were brainwashed to believe that they "weren't shit." This is a phrase that African American people created amongst themselves based on the historical self-fulling prophecies of White Americans claiming that African Americas were second-class citizens. White America did it so well that African Americans believed it and perpetuated this concept amongst themselves and within the community. Because many African Americans put credence to this prophecy, their oppressor finds accuracy in his/her statements, which then further affirms their discriminatory claims. This discriminatory fallacy gives rise to the idea (according to society 's views) that as a people, African Americans ain't shit. If you accept this dogma, then you will ALWAYS have struggles in your life stemming from low self-worth and negative self-perceptions.

But we need to remember, as we say in the African American culture, "God don't make no junk." I come from a mighty creator who gives me infinite intelligence and creativity! As Dennis Kimbro puts it in his text *Think and Grow Rich: A Black Choice*: I am just as worthy of happiness and success as anyone else. *Everyone* was put on this earth to be prosperous and successful. We just need to stop fearing that we are not equal! No matter what your circumstances, you were put on your path to prosper.

Something that really bothers me is when I hear African American people say that White America is holding them back. Society is only going to do what you allow. This is not to say that we can stop people from being discriminating, nor can we force all institutions to be inclusive. But what we have the power to do is get rid of thinking that we will never have anything because White America won't allow it. Change your perception, and your life will change! African American people's fear of racial inequality runs very deep. There are still many people who struggle with reversing and reconditioning their minds from the hundreds of years of brainwashing we endured. African Americans MUST move beyond the life that was historically designed for us to fail.

SANDING AND POLISHING OFF THE MESS

No matter what your race, ethnic background, or religion, changing your self-defeating mindset to one of hope, faith, and abundance is the ONLY way to gain your superpower and live up to the good fortune that you deserve. As Lisa Nichols stated in one of her lectures, "Some of the best motivation comes wrapped in sandpaper." Whatever strife you are going through that is holding you back from your greatness—your SUPERPOWER—can be considered like that sandpaper, the rough and ridged sandpaper that is rubbing you and wearing you down. The more and more you work toward that goal the less rigid that sandpaper will become. Eventually you will be wrapped in a fine grit paper that is no longer wearing on you but is smoothing you out.

Polishing you up and getting rid of the dings, scratches, and imperfections. Your sandpaper can become your saving grace. You know, whenever we go through pains in our life, there is a lesson attached and an opportunity for your character and strength to show up.

My social inequality sandpaper came in the form of me being treated as a second-class academic. I was the only Design faculty at the time who had obtained PhD, though I was still being told I wasn't talented enough—and that really hurt. In the arts fields, a Master of Fine Arts (MFA) counts as a terminal degree, meaning the highest degree that you must obtain in order to become a professor. Most of my colleagues had obtained an MFA, while I did not feel that this was an option for me. As an African American woman, I felt that I had to have a PhD to be considered "equal." And even after I got the PhD, I still had to prove to some of my colleagues that I deserved to be in my position. I deserved to be at one of the best Fashion Schools in the nation because I am one of the best educators.

See, I couldn't get caught up in others' mess that limited others' perceptions of me. I let that affect me for the first 2 years of my professorship, and it nearly killed me. Once I started doing the work I wanted to do and because I wanted to do it, instead of feeling like I had to PROVE myself to a bunch of people who really didn't matter, I unwrapped that sandpaper that Lisa Nichols referred to and emerged as a smoothly polished diamond! Brilliant, clearly cut, and full of grace! There was no stopping me at that point because I was working for MY benefit and to the glory of MY creator, who gave me the gifts to do the job in the first place! Forgive me Lord for doubting you!

CHAPTER 5

FEAR OF
ONE'S OWN BEAUTY

E ven though this chapter is not the last one, it was one
of the last one's that I wrote, because it's hard for me
to talk about. I'm so passionate about this because
aesthetics is my life. The world of beauty and fashion has
been what I've lived for all these years! There is such a
love/hate relationship with me and beauty because of
society's interpretation of what beauty is. Models of African
descent still have to deal with being discriminated against
because of the unspoken fact that, "Black models don't sell
product," according to Vogue Italia; reinforcing the tragedy
that racism is still a major issue in the fashion industry.

Everyone has experienced some feeling of inadequacies
regarding their appearance. No matter if you are the most
beautiful/handsome person on earth, EVERYONE has felt

at some point in their life, felt that they were not attractive enough.

THE WHITE STANDARD OF BEAUTY

I was invited to be the keynote speaker at the Cleveland chapter of the Zonta Club's 2015 Fashion Fundraiser. The title of my speech was, "The Power of Westernized Beauty in the Global Market." In my message I declared that, "External beauty is a visual phenomenon and is therefore exposed to the influences of optical illusions. Optical illusions, meaning lies about what beauty is supposed to be, not what is actually is." I discussed the idea of 'Westernized Beauty,' or as it may be otherwise referred to the 'White Standard of Beauty,' which is defined by being "White, blonde with blue eyes, young, skinny, rich, symmetrical, and abled." Any deviation from these stipulations, the "less attractive" one becomes. International journalist Julie Zelinger says that this beauty standard is coming out of global capitalist structures (in other words, colonization), and is often termed 'whitewashing.'

Fear of one's own beauty is a very controversial topic because it continues to reveal the world's problems caused by most people trying to fit within the White standard of beauty. According to CNN, 90% of Chinese people are getting eye widening surgery. Many in the Chinese society believe that they can get a better job if they have a prettier face as a result of these wider eyes that they pay for. In India, the word for *fair*, meaning light or white, is a synonym for the words meaning *beautiful*, thus Indian women are lightening their skin and straightening their hair. One in three Lebanese and Iranian women have had plastic surgery, according to Elena Rossini, director of the documentary *The Illusionist*. These women are having surgery to get a thinner and straighter nose. Because 80% of women in the middle east wear a hijab; therefore, they want what they actually do show off to be perfect.

Dr. Stephen Marquardt and other researchers have spent a lifetime dissecting the Golden Ratio or *phi* of beauty. This "divine ratio" of 1.618 has been used to explain the proportions of our face shape down to the distance between the location of our eyes and nose. The facial features of people of color often do not match those dictated by the Golden Ratio. They may have a small nose, big lips, or a rounder face structure. Korean women have been known to undergo double-jaw surgery where they have their round Korean jaw removed and replaced with a straighter, more V-shaped chin similar to that of the Westernized Beauty ideal.

More personally, beauty ideas have prolonged the divide within the African American community. Colorism and a term that I have coined, *texturism*, continue to be topics of discussion. Colorism is the societal perception that lighter skin tones are more beautiful than dark ones, while texturism is the societal perception that straight hair is more beautiful than kinky hair. These concepts originated as a result of the Willie Lynch structure that slavery was built on. "Divide and conquer" was the main goal of the master in order to keep his slaves under control.

One of the strategies taught by Wille Lynch involved pitting Blacks against each other by showing preferential treatment to the biracial offspring of the master and his female slave. As we all know, the biracial, lighter skin toned slaves were often allowed to stay in the house, they ate better food, and had access to better clothing. In contrast, the darker skin slaves remained in the fields, ate scraps left over from the house, and were lucky if they had a pair of shoes to wear. This phenomenon created a disturbing intra-racial discrimination that has been perpetuated in Black diasporas all around the world. Under our own doings, this dogma continues to rupture our society 400 years later. The colonialized whitewashing that was forced on Blacks has yet to let up.

QUALMS WITH THE DATING SCENE FOR AFRICAN AMERICAN WOMEN

It has been said over and over that White women are easier to get along with and that they don't give the "attitude" that African American women are so stereotypically famous for. This is a crock, as is the idea that White women are more beautiful and overall more feminine than Black women. Perfect example, Serena Williams one of the best female athletes ever, has been referred to as "manly" and even worst as a "gorilla." The horrible cartoon that was drawn by Mark Knight displayed her as a dark skin animal-like figure jumping up and down in rage.

I was and still am the darkest person in my house. Fear of my own beauty continues to be a sore spot in my mind, from being teased by my younger brother about being adopted, because the rest of my family is a shade or two lighter than me, to being talked about in my youth because I had "nappy" hair. I never had issues with dating as I got older, but I did notice that certain men would never approach me. One jerk I dated in undergraduate had the audacity to tell me that I was the darkest woman he ever dated, as if he was proud to be doing me a favor! And his skin tone was darker than mine—the nerve!! Since the reign of Tinder and other online dating sites, data has shown that Asian men and African American women are the *least* favored to date. In 2017, Eric Francisco published an article entitled *How Tinder Accidentally Exposed Society's Inherent Racism,* and Francisco's article was far from the only one of its kind.

My Asian brothers, I feel your pain and your struggle, but I can't speak to how you may be feeling about this. The variable in your favor is that you are a man, and if you are rich, your "unattractive ways" would somehow vanish and you would be able to pull whoever you wanted. The unfortunate truth is that things just don't work out that way for African American women. With our dark melanin skin and our tightly coiled hair, African American women's level of beauty has been up for debate for centuries! Yes, everybody has at one point in their lives felt inadequate regarding their looks, but among African American women, this dogma runs blood deep. As long as slavery existed, African American women have been brainwashed to believe that they were ugly. Their Master's raped them, while the Master's' wives despised them and often times retaliated by forcing them to cut off all their hair. As a direct result of slavery, African Americans continue to be the only race of people who will coddle their newborn baby and pray that they keep their "good" hair (straight hair) and light skin.

Within the degrading consistency of being told that African Americans (specifically women) were ugly, many of our male counterparts began to also believe the same. According to the 2013 Quartz data, African American women are the least-favored females on dating apps, even being least-favored among African American men whose preference is for Asian and Latina women! Now that's a slap in the face! While I won't get into the reasons behind this in this book, if you do a little research, you'll find some interesting information. I honestly have no problem with interracial dating, but what I have a problem with is people who specifically and purposefully *exclude* their own race of people in their dating repertoire. Self-hate is written all over that! Say what you want, but if you don't find beauty in someone who has similar features as you, then what does that say about you?? Yes, I know what you're gonna say, "here we go again with this topic." But it is necessary to continue talking about this because it is still relevant in today's society. I'll stop talking about it when it is no longer an issue, how about that!

Again, Merton's *self-fulfilling prophecy* comes into play. African American women are being judged by a White standard of beauty as the lesser. Within the African American community, the prophets (African American people) are seeing their predictions coming to fruition. It is extremely dangerous and a total mind-f*ck when people can tell you WHO you are, and YOU believe them and begin living your life according to others' perceptions of you. In that regard, you are giving others control over you. Yes, unbrainwashing takes time and education. When you feel that your level of beauty is not up to par, it is normal and at times inevitable to feel the need to conform. This is with anyone! The White Standard of Beauty reigns over most of the world. However, it is ever present in African American women and all Black women of the diaspora.

SELF-PRESENTION FOR THE PUBLIC VIEW

A fear of one's own beauty is a hard concept to grapple with, and I continue to struggle with it, even in my 40s. I may be a bit different from most because, as I mentioned, aesthetics is my life. I'm a fashion designer for goodness sake, and there is a bit of shallowness that comes with that. I'm not gonna lie, I pride myself in what I wear and how I apply my makeup every day. I refuse to go to the store if I look like I just rolled out of bed. Some of that behavior also shows my level of respect and care for myself.

I'll never forget, a few years ago the Upward Bound Program asked me to come and give a lecture to the high school ladies about dress etiquette. During my presentation, I went into the "dos and don'ts" of dressing for interviews, while on the job, and all-around personal care and hygiene. Well, I got to the part of my presentation when I told the young ladies that real women take pride in the way they look by not wearing a comb stuck in the back of their head or wearing a sleeping bonnet out in public.

What I said really struck a nerve with one young lady in the group and she began to challenge what I said. "So, are you sayin' my mama aint' a real woman? Because she goes to the store with her hair in rollers and a bonnet on her head. I don't see nothing wrong with that!" As she sat there with an attitude on her face and her arms crossed, I went on to say that, "Presenting yourself to the world is of upmost importance. It shows how much you care about yourself." I know that, growing up in the poor inner city, many of these inappropriate behaviors were seen as acceptable. Today, these behaviors are brought to light in a humorous way by being referred to as 'ratchet.' Black people, it is time for us to grow and to move beyond what we have be taught in our communities.

I asked the Upward Bound young ladies, "You want to get a job, right? You want to eventually go to school and have a career, right?" Most of them nodded their heads and raised their hands. I went on to say, "You never know who you will meet in this life that can help you move toward your goals; so when you step out of the house, present yourself in a way that would be appropriate if you met someone who could help you get that job you want. Present yourself in a way that shows people you take pride in yourself. I'm not saying you have to be in a suit but be presentable! As I said before, real women AND men want to display their best selves to the world." I began seeing the ladies' brains churning to process what I just said. As I wrapped up the conversation, I assured myself that some will understand this sooner than others, depending on what type of "home training" they had. As I reflect on my upbringing, I thank God my mom taught my siblings and I manners and how to be respectful to ourselves and others.

A DEEPER ACCEPTANCE OF MY BLACK BEAUTY

In late spring 2019, I ventured to Ghana with a few faculty and a group of students lovingly named the *Intrepid 9* by our trip organizer and professor of Kent State University's Ghana Study tour, Mwatabu Okantah. I tagged along with the group most of the time, but I had also made connections while I was there to meet up with my friend, Dr. Osunyani Essel and his students at the University of Education in Winneba to learn African screen printing and batik techniques. I also wanted the experience of taking a batik workshop with the Global Mama economic co-op, which promotes women earning a living in their respective trades. Global Mamas organizes workshops in bead making, sewing, batik dying, and cooking authentic Ghanaian foods.

First, let me just say, going to Ghana and being in an environment where everyone looks like me was indescribable! The businesses are owned by Black people, the local markets are run by Black people and have local food grown by Black people, AND even the universities are owned by Black people!! My entire life, I have been hard pressed to find an African American that owns anything, including their own house! Maggie Anderson, author of *Our Year Buying Black*, can attest to this same thing. Even rap artist Killer Mike did a rendition of the issues with buying black on his Netflix show, *Trigger Warning*. Some areas in the United States, such as Atlanta, Georgia have a larger number of Blacks who own business; however, there is still a disproportionately low number of Black owned businesses there. The numbers are worse in other cities across the United States.

An immense sense of pride that I never knew was even there came over me, as I watched the hustle and bustle of Black people running their economy. When I came home, I made sure to bring back Ghanaian *cedis* (paper money) for my boys. When I presented them with the money, they looked at me crazy like, "Mom why are you giving me this? You know I can't buy anything with this!" In their confusion, I told them to look at the money. "What's different about this money than the money we have here in the US?" My 10-year-old nonchalantly said, "The people on the money are Black." I responded with, "Yes, this money is very important for you to see. One day we will have a Black person on the bills of the US." [Unfortunately, as of this writing, that dream will be delayed because the United States Treasury has "postponed" the release date of the Harriet Tubman $20 bill until 2028.]

We HAVE to take pride in ourselves as Black people, because if we don't, no one else will. And that starts by changing our perceptions of our value and beauty. If you believe you are beautiful, that comes with so many other attributes such as a high level of self-esteem, which will greatly affect your level of self-efficacy. While staying in the village of Atonkwa, Chief Eduakwa and Chief Whitaker honored myself, the other faculty, and the Intrepid 9 with a naming ceremony. Africans give their children names based on the day of the week they were born. My original birthday is on a Thursday; therefore, my Akan name is Aba or Yaa. I can also combine the names into one, Abayaa. So, my name is Aba Tameka Nicole Ellington. The more I learned about the culture and the way of the tribes, the more connected and prouder I felt.

My last stop before going back home to the United States was to visit with Radford University College, an art school in Accra that boasted being the home of one of the best fashion programs in Ghana, to visit with the Fashion faculty and students. I had been in contact with Nana Kofi Bonsu, a manager at Links Models and fashion photographer for a few years now, and he was my direct connection to Radford. I had done some research on the university and saw images on their website of the facility. I knew I had arrived at the right location when I got out of my Uber and walked up to the front of the five-story building trimmed in orange and blue. I felt an instant connection as I got a closer look at the Radford University College logo, which has embedded in the type the adinkra fern symbol, *Aya*. I am very partial to this symbol because it carries the meaning of resilience and fearlessness. I use *Aya* as a part of the logo for my wellness company, Entirety Incorporated.

Unfortunately, the elevator was not working that day and in the 90+ degree heat I had to climb the steps all the way to the 5th floor, home to the fashion school. I was sweating bullets by the time I got all the way to the top, but I would happily do it again because I was just thrilled to get the opportunity to be there. I was greeted by the lovely Ekua Taylor, director of the Fashion program. We chatted for a moment in her air-conditioned office and then down the hall we went to the students waiting to meet me, the Black American Professor of Fashion (as they called me).

During the tour, the instructors gave me a brief overview of the classes that are offered, which are similar to what we offer our students at Kent State University. Then I was led to a larger lab/lecture type of space where 50+ students were seated waiting to share their work with me. I was offered a seat in the front of the room, and one by one the students stood, introduced themselves, and then talked in detail about their latest design projects. After everyone who wanted to share, spoke; it was my turn to get up and speak. I stood up in front of the jam-packed room, introduced myself and told the students a little about what I do. All of a sudden, my heart started swelling up and my eyes started watering, and I felt an immense amount of peace and joy. As I looked out into the crowd of students, all the words that I had planned to say were lost. I could barely hold myself together, but I managed to gain enough strength to proclaim, "This is the first time EVER in my career, where I have had the privilege to stand in front of a room of ALL beautiful Black faces!" As the tears flowed down my cheeks, the students started to shout with joy!! It was one of the most amazing moments I'd ever experienced! One of the highlights of my career as an academic, for sure!

The next day, it was time to leave Ghana. That was one of the saddest days of my life. I was ready to be back with my husband and my boys, but I was not ready to go back to the United States. I had never in my life felt so welcomed. In the United States I often feel like an impostor when I'm in a room where I am the only Black face. While I was in Ghana, I never felt so beautiful! A couple of men flirted with me while I was there, but it was a different experience because their advances weren't about sex or what I could do for them; it was about trying to get to know me. Let me just say, my husband is lucky that I love him so much! Being in Ghana helped me chip away at that fear of MY beauty not being enough. The pride I gained while journeying to the motherland transformed my chocolate skin and kinky hair into my SUPERPOWERS!

CHAPTER 6

FEAR OF VULNERABLITY: WEAKNESS vs STRENGTH

I remember having a dream a while back that woke me up in tears and in a feeling of despair. A dream about the tug of war of vulnerability and strength.

I was traveling for work and finally arrived at my hotel. The hotel was upscale and elegantly constructed, with tall ceilings and glass windows that were nearly the height of the entire wall. In the restaurant of the hotel, directly over the bar, was beautiful blue velvet fabric that draped from the ceiling over the patrons, to the ceiling at the back of the bar and then down the sides of the walls, making a canopy effect. There was much hustle and bustle in the restaurant, and the food smelled amazing. This dream hotel offered spa showers with steam baths to their guests traveling a long distance who were still waiting to be checked into their rooms. After my long flight I was ready to shower and relax. The concierge gave me a key and began escorting me to my own private shower which was located just beyond the restaurant.

On the way we passed three African American young men; one who appeared to be in his 20s and the other two who appeared to be in their late teens. They began walking up behind me and the concierge. They were trying to slip out of the hotel with merchandise that they just lifted, but they had been discovered by another patron walking by who motioned to the concierge to watch out for the men. The men confronted the concierge. The older one of the men started flexing his muscles and sticking out his chest which then was a prompt for the younger men to pull out the guns they had hidden in their pants. Next thing I know, the young men are pointing a gun at the concierge, and they began escorting him out of the hotel. In my despair I began pleading with the young men to just let the concierge go. The young men couldn't grasp what I was saying, because the older man was yelling and antagonizing the situation. I started pleading louder, "You guys don't have to do this!" I continued to plead, "Please just leave this guy alone! You guys don't have to do this!" As they hurried away from me with the concierge captive, I began wailing!!

I cried myself awake, and the tears I felt while in the dream were now steaming down my face. The first thing that came to my mind as I laid there was "vulnerability." In this case, the young men seemed to be in some form of initiation process. The older man was instructing the younger men on what to do. In their hopes of gaining strength, what the younger men actually gained was a lack of control, and they displayed an immense amount of vulnerability. The young men had lost all sense of wrong and right because they so desperately wanted to impress the older man. Mainly what they are looking for is a way to fill the void they felt in their home life by seeking love, camaraderie, and a sense of strength in a gang. What they don't understand is that through this process, all that is gained is a FALSE sense of love, camaraderie and strength. In actuality, their minds become weak, and they begin to allow others to have power over their thoughts and behaviors.

WEAKNESS - THE VULNERABILITY MOST OF US KNOW

N----s from the hood is the best actors
We the ones that got to wear our face backwards
Put your frown on before they think you soft
Never smile long or take your defense off
Acting tough so much we start to feel hard
Live from the city where they pull cards
I got a Glock 40 and a little nine
Ready for the day a n---a pull mine
N----s from the hood is the best actors
Got learn to speak in ways that's unnatural

Vulnerability has been defined as the fear of being exposed to the possibility of other's inflicted attack or harm, either physically or emotionally. Via this definition, being vulnerable sets you up for what people on the streets call "the wu," in other words, getting played or simply getting something taken away AND getting your feelings hurt in the process. The above stanza is from the song *Washing Clothes* by J. Cole (one of my favorite rappers), where he discusses the fact that African American men cannot go through life carefree; there is a cultural layer of vulnerability that is *forbidden* to be exposed. As a result, they have to ALWAYS be on guard, just in case another African American male decides to "pull their card"— meaning to attempt to physically beat them down or in some cases, murder them. Here J. Cole is breaking down the learned hate (and self-policing) African Americans have for one another, which is an example of the "crab in the barrel" mentality. Constantly being on guard is a way of being that is deeply ingrained in poor, inner-city African American men. This need to feel "hard" is a way to combat societal discrimination that has historically exploited them.

A theory called "Cool Pose" by authors Dr. Richard Majors and Dr. Janet Mancini Billson states that, "For the black male who has limited control or access to conventional power or resources, cool pose is empowering." In this manner "cool pose" means ultimate (perceived) control, slickness, swagger, toughness, all while being well-dressed. It is important to maintain a "cool" exterior, the façade, the mask, the lie—despite the actual internal emotions African American men may have. As a result of 400 years of slavery, 80+ years of lynching and emasculation (where often, men's genitals were cut off in the process) and the racial discrimination that continues today, African Americans (both men and women) suffer from a fear of vulnerability more than their White counterparts.

The need to prove our worth by dressing impeccably has roots in the 1900s. Sociologist and economist Thorstein Veblen's term "conspicuous consumption," or in the slang context "flossing," makes African Americans feel as though they have made it; when in many cases, they can barely afford to keep their lights on. Major corporations such as Nielsen continue to report on the sociological and marketing research regarding the spending habits of African Americans. Directly related to these habits is the tremendous fear African Americans have of not being able to grab their fair share of social and economic capital. The work of Michèle Lamont and Virág Molnár states, "African Americans use consumption to defy racism and share the collective identities most valued in American society,"—status and power. This form of vulnerability has been instilled in the African American culture as a result of mind control and colonialism.

On a larger societal scale, ALL people, no matter their race, suffer from a fear of vulnerability. Men overall suffer from a fear of vulnerability more than women. Traditional gender roles have a considerable influence over this. Males are supposed to be hard, the protectors, and show no emotion, while females are supposed to be soft and submissive; it is almost *expected* for them to be emotional. However, people who have faced societal oppression because of their race, gender, sexuality, ability, or intelligence walk this tight rope everyday of their lives. They are always on guard, waiting for somebody to "play" them or disrespect them, because that is their day-to-day reality. The phrase, "I wish she/he would!" or "Try me!" acts as a warning to others that, "Hey, you may think I'm weak, but watch how I flaunt my SUPERPOWERS." Our sense of feeling vulnerable is directly linked to how we perceive that others see us.

In the professional world, we are seen as unstable if we get upset or cry in the workplace. Maybe you have been going through a tough time at home or your dog just died. Whatever it is, as soon as your colleagues see you in "despair," you are immediately labeled as incapable of doing the work. Unfortunately, it is more socially acceptable to hide your feelings than risk being seen as vulnerable. A fear of appearing vulnerable can show up in many aspects of our lives. This is not just prevalent in the professional world, but it leaks into all forms of social interaction, including our resistance to opening up in platonic and romantic relationships. There are certain situations where we may feel more vulnerable than in other situations.

Personally, my vulnerability fears show up when it comes to money. I have always been a very independent person, and that personality trait started to show up in me as young as 10-12 years old. I never wanted anybody to help me with anything. I hardly asked for help because I didn't like the idea of feeling as though I didn't know what

I was doing. So when I got married, that insecurity crept into my relationship with my husband. According to a recent *Black Enterprise* article, African Americans' personal finances includes high debt, low savings and a lower likelihood of wide financial product (such as stocks) ownership. In turn, the financial disparities and the wealth gap continues.

My mom taught me the basics of how to manage my money. However, when you grow up poor, it's more about stretching the money as far as it can go, rather than actually managing the money. I was always good with paying my bills on time. I wasn't an obsessive shopper, except for every now and again I would splurge on something I really wanted. However, I had accumulated a lot of debt, and I brought that debt with me into my marriage. My husband generously took on my debt in order to help me raise my credit score. Once we got a handle on everything, I went back to managing my own budget and expenses and my husband managed his own. As time went on, I started noticing my debt steadily increasing. The last thing I wanted was to have to ask my husband for help again. I didn't want him to think that I was not capable of taking care of the expenses we agreed I would manage.

In these types of situations our ego takes over because we don't want to appear vulnerable, which in turn, prevents us from getting the help we need. I'll discuss more on the topic of ego later. Having to learn a new skill, and one that is very important such as managing money, becomes a death sentence to our pride. I'm the kind of girl that always wants to appear as though she is in control. When it comes to money, because I didn't have a broad learning experience, I don't know how to properly manage my money, how to save my money and still pay my bills, or how to make my money work for me. Investments: What are those?! (in my Allen Maldonado from *Blackish* voice). Seriously, help me Lord, I have so much to learn. I still struggle with financial literacy today, and I have come to understand that I have to drop my disillusioned strength; in other words, my "cool pose" mask, in order get the financial education I really need. Admitting this, alone, counts as a SUPERPOWER!

SOCIETAL PERCEPTIONS OF A STRONG PERSONALITY

Often times being a person who is driven becomes coupled with that person's fear of appearing too strong to others. Gender roles kick in again here because women suffer with this form of fear more than men. Men are allowed and expected to be the "strength" in the relationship, at work, and all other aspects of our social interaction. They are still considered the most respected members on the gender spectrum; they make the most money and have the better career opportunities.

A 2019 article by A Conscious Rethink, entitled, "13 Signs You Have A Strong Personality That Might Scare Some People," detailed many of the personality characteristics of a person who gets what they want, is successful, stands out in the crowd, and at the same time evokes fear in others. Those characteristics are:

1. You are opinionated and convincing, but not arrogant
2. You are decisive
3. You are led by reason more than emotion
4. You stick to your morals
5. You were not overly concerned with pleasing others
6. You know what you want in life
7. You are very goal oriented
8. You don't dwell on the pass
9. You can actually learn from your mistakes
10. You can admit when you're wrong
11. You are not big on self-pity
12. You seek to understand issues and abhor ignorance
13. You're FEARLESS (I'm sure you know by now this one is my favorite!)

Based on societal perceptions of what it means to have a strong personality, these 13 characteristics align perfectly! However, when we think about gender roles, many of these characteristics are traits that are frowned upon for women. These qualities represent very societal masculine ideas such as, not being big on self-pity or overly concerned with pleasing others. Women, at all times, are to be nurturing— no matter what the situation.

As a professor who's been educating students for more than 15 years, there is often talk regarding research discussing the biases that happen with students' course evaluations of their professors. Gender bias is a major factor especially in male dominated fields. Women are still being referred to as "teacher" instead of "professor," which within itself degrades women's intelligence and capability of managing in a scholarly environment. Let me give a bit of context... Yes, teachers and professors educate students and promoted rigor in their respective pedagogical environments, however in order to be considered a professor, you must attain at least a Master's degree but in most cases a doctoral degree is required. Professors are also charged with conducting scholarly research along with being in the classroom. So, a woman professor being considered a teacher, is an insult.

At times, society's notion of who is strong minded and who is weak is wrapped up in stereotypes. It is expected that men be strong for their families and again the dominate society devalues this quality in women—the Feminist Movement of the 1960s was a means of fighting back against the injustices women dealt with as up-and-coming members of the workforce. This movement fought for women's rights, but in many cases African American women were left out of those efforts. And mainly because African American women were fighting alongside their African American brothers during the Civil Rights movement. As I discussed earlier, intersectionality discrimination is the hand that African American women were dealt because not only were they fighting for human rights as a person of color, but they had to fight to be respected as a woman! So, on the topic of being a person who is considered strong, society expects them to be the meek of the meek! If African American women have an opinion about something, or for even one slight moment show signs of the thirteen characteristics list above, there is a problem. When an African American woman is driven, she is stereotyped as the most strong and aggressive of ALL people! As an African American female, I am well aware of the equation: an African American woman = the "Angry Black Woman." The "Angry Black Woman" stereotype follows African American women into many sectors of our life but is most prominent in our romantic relationships and in the workplace.

In the chapter Fear of One's Own Beauty, I discussed the blasphemous ideology that African American women are harder to get along with than White women. I'm not about to start talking about this 'ish' again! I digress.... In the workplace, it can be damning for an African American woman to have a strong personality and excel at what she does. I know for sure because that was and still is me. Growing up I was a shy young lady; I didn't talk much because when I was a child my opinion was never taken into consideration. But now as an adult, you can't get me to shut up about my perspective on certain situations. In fact, after I filed the Affirmative Action complaint against the Fashion school at Kent State University (I'll talk more about this complaint in the chapter entitled, Fear of Success), one of my colleagues approached me and said, "Do you know everyone (meaning herself) in this department is scared of you." My response was, "Hmmm, I wonder why? Can you please give me some more information on that? I'm not sure what you're talking about because I'm the nicest person anyone could ever want to meet." My colleague's response was, "Well, you know, you were so opinionated about everything and you have such a strong personality. You stand up for yourself (as if I was not supposed to) and you filed that affirmative action complaint. We all know that if there is anything going on in the department that you don't like, you're going to be running up the hill to tell." In that moment, I looked her in the eyes, I had to collect myself and take a deep breath before responding. It took everything in my power not to go off on her. But I politely responded, "Yes, you're right, I am opinionated and that's who I'll always be. *And*, if I didn't file the affirmative action complaint, would I be standing in front of you right now?" She just looked at me dumbfounded. Our offices were right across the hall from each other, so after I said what I had to say, I excused myself, went into my office and shut the door. Once in that safety of my own space, I screamed inside my head, "she is so lucky we are not on 105th and St. Clair! I would've torn her ass a new one!

This stereotype about African American women being strong runs deep within our community's culture. Some African tribes, such as the Ashanti are ruled by a matriarchal standard or have a matrilineage system such as the Akan. African American families often will depend on the eldest mother to maintain family traditions. This woman is often given the name Big Mama or another similar endearing name. In this way, the inner strength that African American women have is needed and appreciated.

Going deeper, this need for African Americans as an ENTIRE race to be strong, takes a toll on our overall mental wellbeing. Of course, this ideology stems from our fight against slavery, like so many other aspects of our lives. The cultural thought process is, "If our ancestors could get through slavery, one of the most horrific of all human indecencies, then we should be able to get through anything with the Lords help." Seeing a therapist to help deal with day to day stress, anxiety, depression, or other situations you may have be going through, frowned upon in the African American community. A saying in the African American community is that "God will fix it!" Yes, God will fix it, by aligning you with the people who can give you the help you need! I'm sure you have heard the phrase, "God helps those who help themselves!" This can be interpreted in so many different ways, but what it boils down to is that we cannot have inner strength all the time on all fronts. We are human, and there is no way we can be strong all the time in all scenarios. It's ok to be vulnerable and ask for help. It's ok not to know ALL the answers ALL the time (I'm telling this to myself too! I admit, I can be wound a bit tight at times!).

In my daily life I suffer from a form of post-traumatic stress disorder (PTSD). Which tends to show up as anxiety and at times depression. The tools I used to fight this are given to me from my doctor and my therapist. I am married to a Psychologist, which has been a very big factor in me seeking help. Another major factor is that one of my mentors, Dr. Angela Neal-Barnett, is a nationally renowned Psychologist who has been featured on the Tom Joyner Morning Show, *The New York Times*, *O Magazine*, and *Essence* (to name a few) for her work on anxiety disorders. I don't know if I would have had the strength to seek out a therapist if I did not have my husband and Angela in my life. I never felt comfortable talking about that to my family because of the self-inflected cultural stigma of mental health in our community. It's funny what you can do in front of an audience (my readers), that you can't do in front of one person. Sorry mom, you have to find out this way!

This societal phenomenon of being fearful that your strength is too much for others, (let's just call them what they are—haters!) comes from the fact that haters just can't handle when someone has self-pride and confidence and believes in excelling at what they do. Haters have an emptiness that just will not allow them to accept another person's fullness. You can't be too strong or too vulnerable. Life's a double-edged sword! How about, you just be your BEST self, and if others can't handle your SUPERPOWERS, that's their problem!

> *"There are 2 types of people who will tell you that you can't make a difference in this world; those who are afraid to try and those who are afraid you will succeed."*
>
> -Ray Gorforth

VULNERABILITY GETS TURNED ON ITS HEAD

What we know of vulnerability is that it's negative, period point blank. It's not a 'good look' to be vulnerable. It's very black and white, Type A... either someone is vulnerable, or they are strong. Many believe that there is no grey here. Professor of Social Work, Dr. Brené Brown's scholarship focuses on attempting to change societies' connation of the word vulnerable. According to Dr. Brown, "We are all looking for a wholehearted life," and the way to achieve that is by being vulnerable with others. During her Ted Talk, she stated that, "Vulnerability is our most accurate measurement of courage." In the next chapter on Fear of Humiliation, Mistakes and Failure, I discuss the dogma and depth of shame. Through her research, Dr. Brown found that shame is really our fear of being disconnected from others. Our fear of shame often times acts as our Fort Knox when it comes to being vulnerable. I am no exception, it took me years to understand that I need others in my life to enrich me, fulfill me and to help me become a better me. Being vulnerable DOES NOT mean we have to be gullible. We know who we can be vulnerable with. Everyone in your life doesn't deserve your highest level of vulnerability, because THEY don't know what to do with it! I have been hurt so much, I only wanted to depend on myself for all things, but I came to understand that this is not sustainable in the long term. I had to reach out, I had to make myself vulnerable in order to reach success! I didn't get my Ph.D. on my own, I had my husband by my side, my most of my professors and classmates cheering me on, and my church family looking to me for the win! Upon graduation, my Pastor asked me to say a few words after the homily regarding my journey in obtaining my Ph.D. This was one of the bible verses that I spoke to the congregation: "For God has destined us not for wrath but for obtaining salvation through our Lord Jesus Christ, who died for us, so that whether we are awake or asleep we may live with him. Therefore, encourage one another and build up each other, as indeed you are doing," (1 Thessalonians 5:9-11).

As human beings, we were first hunter gathers, and this lifestyle mandated that one be connected with a group. For survival on your own was tremendously difficult and almost always was an indicator of your premature death. Nature is a perfect example of that. Animals almost always are connected with a herd, flock, or colony! God created us to be social beings, according to him we HAVE to depend on each other! "Now I beseech you, brethren, by the name of our Lord Jesus Christ, that ye all speak the same thing, and that there be no divisions among you; but that ye be perfectly joined together in the same mind and in the same judgment," 1 Corinthians 1:10. We are ALL a part of God's one body! We ALL breath the same breath blown into our body by God. We are ALL one spirit!

We don't want to surrender to others because we fear something will be taken away from us. Many times, we have been hurt by others, but if we allow those experiences to control us, we will never be fulfilled. We will always live on attack mode and what type of life is that? Trust me, I know all about that miserable life! Our ego can get in the way of our creativity, our dreams our goals and in doing so, stifle us from showing how great we are and how great we can become! When you have the strength to be vulnerable in front of anyone—no matter the circumstances, you possess a power that is supernatural. At that point, you don't care if you will be laughed at, all you want to do is speak your truth. Your vulnerability becomes your SUPERPOWER!

CHAPTER 7

FEAR OF HUMILIATION, MISTAKES, AND FAILURES

" Ego-death—the fear of humiliation, shame, or any other mechanism of profound self-disapproval that threatens the loss of integrity of the Self; the fear of the shattering or disintegration of one's constructed sense of lovability, capability, and worthiness."

- Dr. Karl Albrecht

According to Dr. Karl Albrecht, the five fears that we all share are: 1. Fear of extinction, 2. Fear of mutilation, 3. Fear of the loss of autonomy, 4. Fear of separation/abandonment, and 5. Fear of ego-death. This chapter will touch on the excruciating pain or internal death that humiliation can bring to us. It's almost as if we have died by the hands of others, or even our own hands. Dr. Albrecht discusses ego-death-based fear as the loss of integrity of the self. Wow, this is deep.… An ego-death based fear can lead to a "profound self-disapproval," which for me is the WORST type of fear there is.

Everyone at one point in their life fears being humiliated by others or by some dumb mistake of their own doing. Humiliation is just God's way of keeping us grounded. The old idea of getting "too big for your britches," as my grandmother used to say, just needs a new perspective. How about you humbly create bigger britches and work on filling those? Once those are filled, again create new, even bigger britches and work your ass off to fill those. Don't allow others' fear of your success limit you your potential. The key is HUMILITY, not humiliation. No one can humiliate you if you don't give them power to. Making mistakes will only tarnish your ego if you let it. If you mess up, scream "damn it" a few times to yourself or out loud if that works better for you. Do whatever you need to do to consume a little upset and then move past it with a plan.

MY HUMILIATING TRUTH

In this book, I am sharing some of my truths, but not all. Even I have things that I just can't share yet. You can't put all of yourself out there, just those things that you are brave enough to hold your head up about. Yes, I'm human and still have fears myself. I have come far on my journey, but I am still God's work in progress.

One of the biggest decisions I ever made in my life was to get an abortion when I was an undergraduate. Having the abortion was not a mistake, it was what I needed to do to survive at that time in my life. However, that decision left me with a great deal of humiliation. I remember it like it was yesterday. My friend dropped me off at the clinic because I was not going to be able to drive myself home. As I opened the glass door to the beige brick building, an overwhelming level of grief hit me like a sack of potatoes. The office was sterile looking. The walls were white, the doors were white, and even the worn floor was a dusty shade of white. Almost as if to symbolize that there is no room for life in this space. The receptionist checked me in, and I climbed the steps up to the second floor, pushed past the heavy white door to a waiting room full of other women that were there for the same reason.

Almost every one of the white and gray chairs were filled, but the room was silent. No one exchanged a glance with anyone else; that is, until the big white door opened up again and in waltzed this obnoxious woman. She looked to be about 25 or so. Her hair was stringy and messy; in fact, she looked a bit disheveled from head to toe. She took the seat right next to me and started talking to me as if she didn't have a care in the world. "This your first time here?" she asked me. "Yeah," I answered back dryly. What the hell was she talking about, "first time!?" Yes, this was my first time, and this will be my last I said to myself, as my stomach turned at the thought of having to come back to this place. "Well, this is my fifth time here." I looked at her and shook my head. She then proceeded to tell me about her abortion adventures, until, thank God, the nurse called me back.

Getting the abortion was one of the best decisions I made, but it was also one of the worst things I'd ever had to do. My life would have been so different today. I was a junior in college, and I knew in my spirit that I had a calling for my life, and having a baby right then was not it. Even though I know I made the right decision, it still did not stop that feeling of humiliation from rearing its head. There were only a few people I told about the abortion. I wasn't really ready to talk about it with anyone. Surely not my mother. Our relationship was on the rocks, as it had been since I was about 14 years old. She mentioned to me that I thought I was better than her because now I was in college. There was NO WAY in hell I was going to tell her. I could just hear her now, "See you f*cks up too, just like everybody else." I couldn't have that. So, Mommy, if you are reading this, sorry you had to find out this way.

MISTAKES—THE ORCA'S WAY

Never fret over mistakes, because mistakes are the fortress to your success. If you want to move past your fears, you HAVE to look at it in that way. (Psst, yeah, I know that's easy to say, but not as easy to believe). And if you are a perfectionist like me, it's even harder to believe. You must view your mistakes as growth, even if you work in an environment with sharks that are waiting for you to cut yourself and bleed. Those sharks are even more terrified of being humiliated themselves; therefore, they prey on others' mishaps. Trust me, I know!

As the first and only African American professor of fashion in my department, there were a few of the sharks who tried to block me from my successes by waiting patiently for me to make a mistake. Of course, I made mistakes as I was climbing the academic ladder; however, my successes more than outweighed my mistakes. I have the publications, exhibitions, and awards to prove it! When you do well, maintain an incredible work ethic, and do stellar work, the sharks become a bit intimidated.

Orcas, AKA "killer whales," are the only known natural threat to great white sharks. Great white sharks are known as the head predator (king, if you will) of the seas. However, orcas chase down great white sharks and eat their liver! Now that's some gangster 'ish,' RIGHT?! Orcas are beautiful, graceful, black and white creatures, so beautiful that amusement parks such as Sea World capture them from the wild to train them to perform for paying guests. (That's another topic of discussion for a later date!)

Still, in all their beauty and grace, they have the AUDACITY to be a serious threat to one of the most feared creatures in the world! I say all this to say—be graceful, an image to behold, who just so happens to also be a beast! Be a beast in your field or line of work. Also, in your successes always be humble and thankful for your opportunities and the gifts God gave you. With that combination, the sharks can't touch you; as a matter of fact, they will run from you because you will eat their livers for dinner!

FAILURE–ONE OF THE BOLDEST FORMS OF REJECTION

"Failure is another steppingstone to greatness." These wise words from Oprah Winfrey help us understand that people who are successful in any arena have gone through failures. However, when our failures are tied to others' thoughts about us, it can look a lot like rejection. In a 2013 article in Psychology Today, several aspects of rejection are broken down into dimensions: the natural origin of rejection, physical pain caused by rejection, emotional pain caused by rejection, and behavior reactions to being rejected.

We can relive and re-experience social pain more vividly than we can physical pain. In our hunter gatherer past being ostracized from our tribes was akin to a death sentence because no one could survive on their own. Still today, our brain prioritizes (puts at the forefront of our mind) rejection experiences because we are social animals who need to live in and belong to a group. Also, according Psychology Today, feeling alone and disconnected after a failed relationship that resulted in being rejected by others can cause anger and aggression, as well as destroy our self-esteem.

It can be hard to feel rejection at work, but especially in your personal life. Maybe you worked hard and did not get the promotion. In our minds this equates to failure which is a direct connection to rejection. My tough relationship with my mother in many ways stemmed from the fact that I felt rejected by her. In one of his sermons, Pastor T.D. Jakes proclaimed, "When people can walk away from you, let them walk." In a situation where you have a failed relationship that has resulted from someone you loved abandoning you, you have to let that go. In friendships it's rough, especially when you really love your friend and enjoy their company.

I had a situation where I felt like I was constantly chasing one of my friends. I valued her friendship so much that I could not bear to lose her. After more than 2 years of trying to reconnect with her, and the heart wrenching humiliation that these failed attempts brought on, I finally developed the strength to just let it be. Some days I still think about how close we were; but I have to keep reminding myself, I did nothing wrong. She just evolved— and in that evolution, our friendship was not a part of the plan, and that's ok. Many times, when we have feelings of rejection those feelings can cause us to make irrational decisions. Hence, why I tried for two years to work on a friendship with no reciprocating effort on my friend's part.

In marriages, I have heard, that it can be humiliating to be "left" by your spouse. One of my mentors had her husband walk out on her. She told me that she was not ready to get divorced and how humiliated she felt because of this failure in her life. In the next few years, she met another man, fell in love, remarried, and she was happier than she had ever been. Her new husband's generous and kind nature was the total opposite from the nasty disposition of her previous husband. Failures are many times Gods way of taking us through the grinder so that we can come out on the other side a polished gemstone.

When I first became a professor and had to start putting my design work and my research publications out into the field, I was terrified!! I was fearful that my colleagues wouldn't like my work and that they wouldn't get my perspective. Well, I soon learned that being in academia, you get lots of rejections. Submitting exhibition work and getting rejected or submitting an article to a journal and getting rejected is a way of life. It sucks, but it's how you play the game. You correct some parts based on the feedback from the reviewers, and you just find another exhibition or another journal to submit your work to. Eventually, you will get picked up. The first time I wrote a grant proposal to get federal money for a project, it 'bout nearly took the wind out of me.

My research partner and I put our heart and soul into that proposal, and it came back rejected. We went through the reviewers' comments with a fine-tooth comb and resubmitted a year later; just to get rejected again. Man, that hurts my heart every time I think about it. However, we decided to change up our way of thinking—we strategized and submitted our proposal to a foundation instead. We were awarded the money to be able to make our project happen. If at first you don't succeed, try and try again, and then again if you have to. One of my good friends who has been a very successful grant writer told me, "Well you got rejected that time, it just makes more room for when the yeses start coming in!" The GLORY in trying is that you won't ever have regrets that you didn't give it a shot.

So, humiliation, mistakes, and failures are a way of life. It's how we learn and stay grounded. God has placed tribulations in our lives to help us learn to strategize and do better. Like the saying, "when you know better, you do better." If that "knowing better" simultaneously fosters maturity and wisdom; then yes—you won't make the same mistakes twice. And the next time you make a mistake, you will have a different perspective about it. It's not dooms day—it's time to bust your ass and/or clear your mind to make sure it doesn't happen again.

CHAPTER 8

FEAR OF SUCCESS

D o you deserve to have an abundant life? Be wealthy? Be happy? Yeah, only if you can talk White and not be too ghetto. This is a joke... but not really.

TALKING "PROPER"

I was always a bit different than the other kids in my neighborhood. My mother taught us plain English and only allowed us to speak that way in her house. She used to say to us, "there's no such thing as the word ain't!" I was always a smart kid; I loved school and once I started primary school, I came home and taught my little sister everything I knew. She actually entered the 2nd grade as a gifted and talented student, thanks to my teaching!

Being smart was not something that was popular in the inner city, but for me books were my way to escape the ghetto madness. My mother told me that there was many a day I would stay in the house reading or drawing while my brother and sister went outside to play. Reading made me happy and allowed me to visualize a life that was different from my reality. So, speaking "proper English" came along with being a well-read child. My little brother and my friends would always say that I talked "proper." Even some of my mother's friends that visited our house would tease me about talking "proper." Basically, what talking "proper" meant is that I was talking like a White person. It used to bother me that I spoke differently than my peers, and so I learned at an early age that it became mandatory for me to codeswitch. I needed to fit in, so that I didn't stand out too much.

I always prided myself on being able to be "bilingual," as Michelle Obama put it in her *Becoming* book tour interview with Oprah. She discussed the need to move between two worlds: the White world and the world of her south-side Chicago neighborhood. Being accused of talking White or talking "proper" is a stigma that many educated African Americans have to deal with from within our own community. It is truly a form of intercultural racism: the crab-in-a-barrel mentality I spoke about earlier, that unfortunately many African Americans still have against each other. I believe that has been a definite curse to our race and one of the reasons why we can't seem to break out of our communities' generational curse of poverty. As we become more educated, we can begin to understand the need to have a *double consciousness*, as W.E.B. DuBois coined. In order to survive, we have to know when to turn

the ghetto off. After much practice, codeswitching becomes
second nature. The whole purpose of educating ourselves is
so that we can see a different way of life. Even if it means
we have to appear as "someone else" so that others aren't
threatened.

But when you think about it, although it may start out
as a reaction to external circumstances, when you expand
yourself in this way, you are becoming an evolved you, a
more well-rounded you, a you who will know how to move
between various spaces. Are you selling out? Hell no! You
are bringing your culture up and advancing your culture by
educating yourself. You gaining abundance is not a
detriment to your status in the hood.

Don't let them fools fool you into thinking that you left
your prior legacy as an African American when you
crossed the graduation stage! The best thing you can do is
get some abundance and come back to the hood and share
that with others to help them grow into their own
abundance. And let me be clear—abundance is not just
wealth; it is living in an environment where you don't have
to feel threatened or on guard when you step outside your
front door. Abundance is living a life of peace and
happiness and only allowing others into your life who are
at peace with themselves and project the positive energy
you need to maintain your abundant life. So, talk "proper"
all day long…while walking into your abundance.
Abundance begins with educating yourself. It doesn't
necessarily have to be a formal education like mine, but

growing your knowledge is important no matter how you go about it.

MY JOURNEY INTO THE ACADEMY

I remember when I was on the journey of completing my PhD, it was some of the most intense times in my life!! My body was so stressed, I contracted shingles at the age of 34! I literally did not think I was going to finish. The dissertation edits alone I thought would kill me, and on top of that I had a new baby boy who needed my attention. I had to miss my son's 2nd birthday because I had stinking edits to get done! The thought of that makes me want to cry, but I had to be strong and sacrifice to make major change in my life.

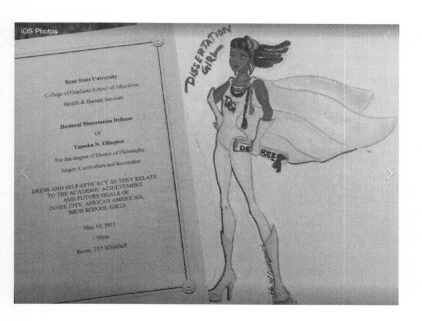

I needed some motivation, and so I drew a superhero who I called Dissertation Girl, and I posted her to my office door. She was wearing a yellow leotard with an electric blue tam (doctoral graduation hat) and blue and gold Honors cords. Every time I walked into my office, Dissertation Girl was in my face. Seeing her with her diploma in her hand put me into the "now or never" mindset. I'm not a quitter, and I had to coach myself. I had to finish this PhD even though my dissertation committee became short one person 5 days before I was going to defend! I also had to ask one of the professors on my dissertation committee to step down because he was slowing up my progress! He wasn't offering me any help and was just making things difficult for me and the others on my committee. If you have been on this journey, you know how much pressure that can be and how you have to have SUPERPOWERS to be bold enough to kick a professor off your dissertation committee!

There was a time in my life when I feared I would not find my place in any workforce that could make me happy. When I finally found my place, I could barely get in without having to fight. Being an educator became my life's calling. As I mentioned earlier, I got my first opportunity to teach as a graduate student at Michigan State University. Once I got into it, things just flowed. It was like I was born to teach.

After I completed my Master's at Michigan State, I wasn't quite sure that education was the path that I wanted to go down, because I had a fear that I would not make much money as an educator. By this time, I had been out of undergraduate for about five years, and my classmates had continued working in the fashion industry and were making great money. Many people think that fashion is not a viable major to study or for an actual career; little do they know that there's lots of money to be made.

I always hate it when I have aspiring Fashion students of mine tell me that their mother or father made them choose nursing, or accounting, instead of Fashion. They always say their parents are afraid they won't be able to get a job. But we wear clothes every day, and trends change and are cyclical. People will always need clothes, and many people want fashionable clothes. So yes, the fashion industry is a viable major where students can earn a great living. Knowing that, my friends who were still in the industry thought I was insane for wanting to go back to school, get a Master's degree, and teach. I had a number of them tell me "Girl, you gon' be broke!" All my life up until that point, my mission was to get myself out of poverty. So, of course I decided not to go into the teaching field where I "knew" I wasn't going to be able to make much money. Fear sent me back into the fashion industry after completing my Master's.

In the fashion industry you don't need a Master's degree or any kind of graduate degree to get a position. Most jobs require a four-year degree, talent, and a high work ethic. When I started going on interviews to find a job, and I had a number of potential employers ask me, "So why did you

get your Master's degree?" as if it was a bad thing. I always
came back with the rebuttal that education was extremely
important to me because I had been the only person in my
immediate family to complete a four-year degree. I always
felt I had to set the standard for my siblings because I was
the oldest. Yes, this was true, I did (and still do) value
education. But let's not get it twisted, for real for real—
prior to starting my Master's, I was in and out of jobs that
were not a good fit for me and constantly left me feeling
empty. Getting my Master's degree was a way for me to
have a positive holding pattern until I could figure out what
the hell I was supposed to be doing with my life!

I began working as a designer for the big brand
Abercrombie and Fitch at their New Albany (suburb of
Columbus, Ohio) headquarters. I loved what I was doing
for the first time in my life! I was making great money, and
I was happy with the work I was producing. After a while,
though, that empty feeling began to overtake me once
again. I began to wonder and daydream about whether this
was really where I was supposed to be. Yes, I was working
as a designer. Yes, I was doing what I was trained to do—
make cool product. But I still wasn't happy. Going into
work was fun, but it didn't give me JOY! When I mean joy,
I mean the peace of mind that you get when you know you
are doing what your creator sent you here to do. By joy, I
mean a happiness that brings about great satisfaction in
that you are contributing something powerful to the
universe. I just didn't feel that way. After leaving
Abercrombie and Fitch, I went and worked for a small
women's catalog company, called J. Marco Galleries, where

I ran their design department, and I had five Assistant Designers working under me.

After about a year into this position, that empty feeling started to creep back up. Once again, I felt like I didn't know what the hell God sent me into this world to do. Author and entrepreneur Dennis Kimbro states that the best thing is when you understand who you are and why you were sent here. Much of my uncertainty left me feeling purposeless about the work I was doing. I had gone to school and gotten two degrees in design. I couldn't image working in another field. What the hell else was I supposed to do?!

I discovered that I was sent to educate others. I often reflected back to my time in the classroom teaching at Michigan State and wondered if I could do that for a living. God sort of pushed me in that direction because there were not many fashion design companies in the Cleveland area, and so, my options were limited. I started teaching part-time at Kent State University, in The Fashion School. I was 27 years old, and my husband and I had just gotten married. I was ready to start having children. So, teaching part-time was an ideal situation for being a mother. I was making no money, but I would be able to take care of my future babies without them having to go to childcare. At that time, my husband was in school for his PhD in Psychology, and he knew how frustrated I had been with my career situation. He suggested that I get a PhD.

I was not feeling getting a PhD because like I said, I was ready to start having babies. In my family, if you haven't had your first child by a certain age (usually in your early 20s), it meant that you couldn't get pregnant! My younger cousin, who by the time she was 27-28, she had 3 babies actually, asked me if I could get pregnant. I told her I wasn't trying because Aaron and I had just gotten married, and I didn't have my career where I wanted it to be. She just couldn't wrap her head around that situation. My mother told me I was going to be old and grey before I had my first child. That's just more typical inner-city thinking.

Another reason I didn't want to get the PhD is because I didn't know which major to study. The closest school that had a PhD in Apparel and Textiles was The Ohio State University, and we lived two hours away. For someone like me who hates driving, that was not even an option! A friend of mine who taught at The Fashion School was working on her PhD in Curriculum Studies. Her entire career had been in fashion retail, and she told me about how much she liked the program.

Most important was the third reason I didn't want to go for my PhD—FEAR! A past boyfriend that I had been with for 6 years (before I met my husband) had been everything to me, but he was also very insecure and immature. I was in school for my Master's toward the later part of our relationship. When I made the decision to go to school, I told him I was accepted at Michigan State University and that I would be moving for school. He had just finished his undergraduate degree about 4 years prior and was floating in a purgatory trying to figure out his life, so he decided to come with me. His retail management job was able to get him a transfer to Lansing, Michigan. In July 2002, he and I headed to the MI. We always got along well, and I thought that I was going to marry this man. I even bought him a "promise" ring to try to get the ball rolling on him asking me to marry him. (Yeah, that ish never happened!)

The issues started once I had gotten acclimated into school, and I was doing very well. I was making friends and gaining recognition amongst my peers and my professors. I started getting invited to important events on campus, such as being asked to be a judge for the undergraduate student senior-year fashion show. I got two free tickets to the show, and of course I invited my boyfriend. He got to see firsthand how much everyone loved and respected me and that made him jealous. A friend of mine I had met in Lansing was studying for her Actuary exams, so she and I decided to start studying together. I would spend almost every Sunday at her house, or we would go to the library to work. My boyfriend, in his jealousy, accused me of having a romantic relationship with her. What he was really doing was reflecting his cheating-ass guilt and insecurities onto me. Sometime later, I had expressed to him that I was really enjoying being in school and was thinking of continuing through for my PhD. He looked me dead in the eyes and told me, "Well, there's no way I could ever marry a woman who has a PhD if I only have a Bachelor's degree."

I found myself trying to tame my achievements in order to make him feel better about himself. I tried to talk myself out of furthering my education, saying to myself, "Well, I really don't need a PhD; I don't think I could do it anyway because the curriculum requires lots of statistics and I'm not good at stats." The foolish things we do when we love someone!! It got to a point where I could not even come home and tell him about the wonderful experiences that I was having at school. That was the final straw for me, and I broke off the relationship. But by that time, I had already psyched myself into believing I wasn't smart enough to get PhD; therefore, it became the furthest thing from my mind until I met my husband, who encouraged me to go for it.

I made a pact with my husband that I would apply for the PhD program in Curriculum and Instruction, and if I didn't get in, we would start having babies. The agreement was that, if I did get in, we would wait a few more years. So, I half-ass applied. I have always loved writing, and I wrote a bomb research and personal statement, which did it! To my dismay, I got accepted., but it turned out that being a PhD student was the most intellectually invigorating times in my life! I was in school with a bunch of K-12 educators, and I was the only fashion person in my cohort. I was the creative thinker in my group, and I loved it! I worked hard and graduated with a 3.94 GPA and was inducted into the Alpha Kappa Mu Honors Society. The society was created to honor, promote, and reward academic excellence among African American students.

While I was in school for my PhD, I taught part-time at my beloved Kent State University Fashion School. During my stint as a part-time instructor, three full-time non-

Tenure Track (NTT) positions became open. I applied for all three of those positions, and I got turned down for all three. I kept noticing that the individuals that were given the positions had less education than I did. I noticed it the first time around, then again, the second time around, and then finally, the third time around. By this time, I was devastated and heartbroken because I bleed blue and gold!! How could the school director keep passing me up for people who had less education than me?

I literally had one of my colleagues (who soon after had left the university, thank God!) tell me that I would never get hired full-time because The Fashion School already had their "token Black girl." WOW! To may face! I'm usually pretty bold and will have a comeback, but I was just in shock! What do you say after some 'ish' like that!? All three of the individuals who were given the full-time job that I applied for were White women, which infuriated me even more. I went and spoke with a mentor of mine about the situation, and she took me directly to the campus director of the RECC (Race and Ethical Concerns Committee). He and another professor helped me file an Affirmative Action complaint against The Fashion School. Then with a wave of a wand, I magically got an NTT full-time job.

Once I completed my PhD I went to my director at The Fashion School and said to him, "The Fashion School has never had an African American Professor, I think it's time." He replied, "I couldn't agree more!" He and I put together a proposal that we presented to my colleagues. I was going to be the first person in my department to apply for what the

university called a "position waiver." The position waiver
would allow a full-time NTT instructor to apply for a full-
time Tenure Track (TT) professor position. It is very rare
to have a position waiver be accepted at our university, but
my God told me that anything was possible.

Now, I must give some context here before I continue.
As I stated earlier, I started out as a part-time, adjunct
instructor at The Fashion School. At that time, the school
was headed up by another director who has since passed on
due to her battle with cancer. She was a small, cute lady
who had a southern drawl from her upbringing in North
Carolina. She was the same director who was there when I
was an undergraduate, so I knew her very well. I had even
gone to visit her in the hospital during one of her cancer
recurrence phases. Before I had come to work for The
Fashion School, I was working for Abercrombie and Fitch
as a Technical Designer (TD). The director was in the
process of developing a new curriculum for technical
design, so she found me, called me up, and asked me some
questions about important elements that she should add to
the curriculum. Of course, I didn't hesitate to teach her all I
knew about TD and the manufacturing business.
Coincidently, a little over a year later, I ended up coming to
The Fashion School to teach part-time because I had left
Columbus to be closer to my husband. This same director
was running the department when I applied for the three
NTT positions. I was good enough to get information from
and consult with (for free), but not good enough to hire
full-time.

Now with my PhD completed, the new director submitted a position waiver for me (with an unfortunate disapproval of some my colleagues), and I became The Fashion School's first African American professor! Some of my colleagues really had a tough time with it. "She is not talented enough to be a professor here," some said. "She is going to need ALL of this mentoring that we just can't give her," others said. All of this chatter came from people even though, as one of the many tenure-track Fashion Design professors, I was the ONLY damn one who had a PhD!

In Fashion and most other Art disciplines, a Master of Fine Arts (MFA) is considered a terminal degree (highest you can go). I knew that there was NO WAY I could get a position as a professor if I only had an MFA. I had to be better and have more education in order to get the same level of opportunities as White professors.

Now in my new role, I had to come to work with people who did not want me there. I began to become very self-conscious about my design, research, and teaching abilities. It was almost as if those people had gotten into my head and changed my mind about who I knew myself to be. The self-fulfilling prophecy kicked in, and I became very afraid to put my work out into the field for others to criticize. I allowed my colleagues to remain "in my head" for the first two years while I was on the tenure track. During that time, my youngest baby had a spontaneous rupture in his lungs and nearly died when he was just 4 weeks old. Through divine intervention and great health care (thanks to my son's Pulmonologist and my homegirl, Dr. Strawbridge), he lived and became a strong little boy! If my baby boy can endure and come out on top, so could I. My days of grimacing under my colleagues' perceptions of me was OVER!

My fear that I would not be good enough and the thought of proving my colleagues right became my fire— my SUPERPOWER! I used to hunker down in my office and seep in those negative comments made about me. It literally made me crazy! The stress was REAL! My body started reacting, and I found bald spots on both sides of my head, which of course sent me into a panic. I began eating to cope with my stress. When I would get really upset, I would just break out with, "I need some chocolate cake" and then be on the hunt to find some.

I had been doing a lot of praying about the situation. I would say these quick, short prayers: "Lord give me the strength and wherewithal to face these people today." "Lord give me the creativity and the skill to make the best art that I can." And "Lord, thank you for all the gifts you have given me, please continue to flow through me and improve me." After a while, I began not to care what my colleagues thought. I was all about pleasing me and my creator. It was like I had an invisible sticker on my forehead that said "Kiss my black a**!" LOL, I often envisioned that sticker on my head when I was dealing with certain colleagues. I now had my SUPERPOWER and I was off to the races!! NOTHING or NO ONE was going to stop me. I became a beast and one of the most highly regarded researchers in my field. Yeah that's INTERNATIONALLY, biiiitttchessss!!

FEAR OF OTHERS' SUCCESSES

When it comes to success, never measure yours against another's! You will lose your mind trying to keep up with "the Jones's." Your journey is different than anyone else's. Only you are the expert on your capabilities and talents. What might be the missing link is your fear that you won't have what it takes. If you want persistence and resilience in your life, compounded with your capabilities and talents, look for that WITHIN! No one can give you that and being in direct or indirect competition with someone will constantly leave you feeling inadequate. You do YOU!! You be the best example for your success, whatever that looks like to you.

My philosophy is that I'm not competing with anyone. I am doing my best and I would hope that others are doing their best. No one can do what I do! Nor can anyone think or feel the way that I think or feel, so there is no possible way that I can be in competition with someone who is nothing like me! We are all special in our own way! Be your special self and the rest will fall into place.

Fear of someone else's success out-measuring yours will lead to nothing but jealousy and envy. It will hurt your heart and pride every time. Now, this is not to say you can't have people who you admire and who you might model your life after, but keep in mind YOUR journey and the path God put YOU on! I highly doubt He instructed you to work to be better than such and such; or work to outdo this person or that. He has called you to be the best at what it is YOU do!!

Recently I had a terrible heartbreak from a purposeful dissolution of a friendship with my VERY BEST friend. I still love her but, as my husband says, I just had to "recategorize our friendship." Man, that sucks, but it is what it is! I started noticing a difference in our relationship after I had left Ohio to attend Michigan State University to get my Master's degree. She and I talked on the phone often and easily maintained our friendship as if I was still just right down the street from her. However, one day during our conversation her jealousy towards my accomplishments started to become quite plain. At the time I had been dating my then-boyfriend for over five years. We had moved in together, and I was ready to take our relationship to the next level. However, my boyfriend was not ready. Whenever we would talk about it, he would always push things off, push things to the side and not really give me a definite answer.

My BFF and I grew up together throughout elementary and high school; she was one of my oldest friends. I remember she and I would go bike riding and be gone 6-8 hours at a time, riding all over Cleveland. Her family was like my family and vice versa. She became my little sister's "big sister" when I left for college. She looked after my little sister and helped to keep her out of trouble. I could always depend on her, and we always had so much fun together.

As we got older our lives began to drift apart. It was like we didn't know each other anymore. The person I was the most comfortable around my whole life, became a person I felt like I couldn't share my secrets, my dreams and my aspirations with.

One day I was on the phone with my her, in tears giving her the whole rundown. Once I finish venting and the tears started drying up, a strange silence fell on the conversation. She said in a low cynical voice, "Huh, I didn't think you wanted to get married. Seems like you're so busy with your career and school. I couldn't see you wanting a family." By this time my BFF had a beautiful little boy with a man who had gone and impregnated two other women prior to my BFF's son being born; therefore, she had become a single mother by the time we were 21 years old. She decided not to go to college and was holding onto some resentfulness. I was devasted! "How could you say that!" I yelled at her. "You've known the names that I have picked out for my kids since we were in high school! Why would you say that!?" I couldn't understand how my BFF could possibly be jealous of me. Friends aren't supposed to do that! Especially sisters! After that conversation, we did not talk for a few months. That incident started the downward spiral of our friendship.

Recently, my family and I were on our way to a vacation in the Smoky mountains. We decided to cut the drive time into two days, and so I asked my husband if we could plan our stop in my BFF's state. I had not seen her in over 5 years and so I was ecstatic about the possibility to see her.

After a long day of driving we arrived at the hotel where my BFF was going to be meeting us. When she arrived and came up to our hotel room, a barrage of emotions ran through me: excitement and nervousness all at the same time. I didn't quite know what to expect since I hadn't seen her in so long. On top of that, we just didn't talk as much as we used to.

When I open the door, I was thrilled that she looked great. I knew she had been struggling with her weight for the past couple years. And it looked like she lost much of the weight she had gained plus some. Her makeup was always flawless—that was something she was great at. She came into our hotel room and gave my husband a hug and said hi to my boys. And then she and I went down to the lobby to spend some time together.

The conversation started out with us catching each other up about our families. As we talked further, the conversation took a very unusual direction. Of course, I told her about all the wonderful things that had been going on, as well as some of the things that were not so great. She already had much of the details about my career because I post my work activities on Facebook. Unfortunately, her life had not progressed much. Her son was an adult now, driving and taking care of himself. She was still struggling with securing work. She had started on the journey of becoming a minister, which was a little bit surprising to me. Being a path to become a minister takes so much passion, dedication, and commitment. For many years my BFF had a really difficult time staying the course at any of her goals. It became disheartening for me to see her unhappy most of the time.

As I continued to talk to her about some of the challenges I'd been having, she began coaching me and rattling off scriptures to me, which felt very unauthentic and rehearsed. She started preaching to me, "You are special, you are a child of God…." I was kind of in shock, I didn't quite know what to say. I had never seen her in this capacity before, and I hate being preached at. Then we started talking in more detail how I've been able to successfully move through my career even with the challenges I faced.

Again, regrettably, my BFF had never really found her calling. She decided not to go to college, and she bounced from job to job. It broke my heart to see her struggling. So as I completed the conversation about my works; she responded, "I see that your career is going very well and you're doing big things! But what about your marriage, how are you and your husband?" Now, I always made it a point not to share and intimate details about my husband to my single friends. In my experience, single friends just can't give sound advice to their married friends because they have never been in that situation.

I told her that we were doing well, but of course no relationship is perfect. I was telling her about the few minor bumps my husband and I had here and there. I refused to share any major complications my husband and I were going through. Finally, she had the nerve to say, "Well it's funny that you say that (in regard to the minor issues I shared), because I had a dream about you." She continued, "In my dream I saw that your career was going fantastic, but your marriage was in shambles." Then, oddly, she started consoling me, "Weeeelll, everything can't be perfect!"

The strangest, strangest feeling came over me. As I sat there staring at her, I came to realize that she was *looking* for something to be wrong with me! She was looking for my flaws! Instead of being like a true friend should be, with comforting words, her words were trying to break me down. In the past, I remembered these sorts of destructive comments coming from her, but not to this extreme! As we finished our conversation, my heart started to break. It became clear to me that I had to remove her from my life. We got up from the table, and I gave her a stale hug. It was as if I was in a trance. I pushed the button to the elevator to go back up to my room. As I walked down the hall, I could barely lift my feet. I got to the door and slowly pushed the key card into the lock. As I opened the door, I looked at my husband with a sad expression and said, "I never want to talk to her again."

During a keynote lecture called *Courageous Conversations on Race*, Dr. George Fraser talked about his famous friends who helped to change the scope of our nation. His list included the likes of Malcolm X, Dr. Martin Luther King Jr., and Oprah, who all had one simple secret in common: "They have the ability to remove toxic people and blood suckers from their lives." He goes to explain that less successful people have not been able to do this, and they allow others to pull them down and prevent them from growing. He explains that many of us have a hard time doing this because oftentimes those individuals are our family. My BFF was like my sister and having to remove her from my immediate circle hurt like hell!

THE FIRST-GEN SUCCESS NIGHTMARE

This last type of fear of success is quite haunting and isolating. It is the type of fear that will keep you down in the dumps and make you resentful. Some of you other first-generation revolutionaries know what it's like to be the only "success" in your family. Meaning that you're the only one making a decent living, and from the outside looking in others think you are "rich" because you don't need government assistance of any kind. With this success comes the responsibility of helping others in your family.

When my little sister went to college, I was thrilled for her. She was going to be the second person in our family to earn a degree. She followed in my footsteps and went to Kent State University. I was elated because I still lived about 20 minutes away from the campus at that time, so she and I could hang out much more. To help her get on her feet, I decided to co-sign to help her get a car. It was my pleasure to be able to do that for my sister; I wanted to give her the assistance I didn't have when I first started out.

Well, my sister got to school and loved it! Towards the later part of her first semester, though, she had a situation with one of the White girls on her floor. The girl was antagonizing my sister, and my sister tried to keep her cool. I had explained before she even came to college that the environment is not the same as back home. Especially with her being at a Predominately White Institution (PWI); if you fight, you get kicked out, simple as that. The White girl on my sister's floor got huffy with my sister and then commenced to put her hands on my sister. That was the wrong thing to do! Being from the inner-city and having to fight for survival, you get accustomed to fighting. So, my sister did what she would have done had she been back at home on St. Clair Avenue, she beat the girl's ass! Well, of course, the girl ran to the RA, and to make a long story short (and to speed this up because I hate talking about it), my sister got kicked out, while the White girl was allowed to remain in college.

My sister was devastated and washed her hands of college. She was through! She was working at a job and making decent money in order to help maintain the car note, but then she ended up getting pregnant and got into some legal troubles. She ended up not being able to maintain the note, and the car got repossessed. Since I was the co-signer, the bank came after me for the money. I ended up having to pay $5,000 to the bank in order to clear both of our names; however, the repossession still showed up on my credit report! After that incident, I promised myself that I wouldn't do that anymore. A few years later, my mother asked me to co-sign for her and I hated to tell her no, but I had to protect my own credit. A few years later, my brother wanted to buy his first house, and he

came to me to borrow the money. I was thankful to be in a
position to be able to help him, but who was going to help
me?

I began to be fearful of getting any more successful than
I had attained. I was afraid that my family would take
advantage of me. Or just expect for me to pay for things. I
learned how to set boundaries, and things got better. After
some time, I just realized that this fear was a silly reason to
hold myself back. It was downright selfish! My goal became
not only to help get myself out of poverty, but to also help
my family break the curse of generational poverty.

God spoke into my life the endless possibilities in front
of me and my family. This became my SUPERPOWER!
The dream of having the power to change the trajectory of
my family's ancestral financial blueprint has been my
inspiration. If I win, I have to help my family win. If I can
change their minds' perceptions about their own potential
by being an example of what success looks like; then
together, WE can pull OUR family out of the ghetto trap.

My new mission is to spread my SUPERPOWERS over
my family! If ALL people living with a generational curse of
poverty—no matter your race—could gain some self-worth
and some SUPERPOWERS, our world would be a different
place. Violent crime would decrease, people would not be
hungry, and we could have an overall happier, loving
existence. I aspire big! Dreaming has no action but aspiring
to do something puts thoughts into motion! I plan to
change the world, one soul at a time.

CHAPTER 9

FEAR OF THE UNKNOWN

In 2016 I was accepted into an exhibition in Beijing, China. I was very excited for the opportunity to venture to China. But I kept my future journey from my mother for months. My mom has never flown on an airplane and she has never been in the car for long distances. The number of times she's been out of Ohio can be counted on one hand. There was no way I was going to tell her that I was going to China, because I knew she would try to talk me out of it! Growing up in the inner city also limits your perceptions of how big and wide the world really is.

Oh boy, and Clevelanders driving 'cross town' meant driving 15-20 mins from one area of the city to another. Never did many dare leave the proximity of their neighborhoods. Like I said in the beginning of the book, Cleveland is one of the most segregated cities in all of the United States. The East-siders and the West-siders, never shall the twain meet. That fact is of course due to classism and racism, but it is also partly because nobody wants to drive far enough to get across the Hope Memorial Lorain-Carnegie Bridge!

Three days before it was time for me to leave, I finally called my mom and told her that I was on my way to China. Of course, just like I knew she would, the first thing she said was "aren't you scared to go all the way over there?" In response I told her, "if I'm going to die on the plane, at least I would have been doing something that I've always wanted to do."

A fear of the unknown can keep us from doing many of the things we were destined, or as some say, "called" to do. Some people may be afraid to go to a different country, some may be afraid to go to school to get educated for fear that they won't be smart enough, and most people have a fear of what they don't know and don't understand. Racism is a prime example of that.

When you have a calling on your life, it is truly a sin not to listen and act on that call. The universe gives everyone a talent, and some of us are lucky to have more than one! If you are not sharing those talents because you have a fear of the unknown, you are literally wasting your life! No one has your creative gifts, no one can do what you do because you were uniquely and divinely birthed into this world. Think about all the people who won't get to see your greatness if you stay affixed to only the things you KNOW about.

On a more spiritual level, everyone was created by the almighty, and he automatically equips us with the necessary tools we need for living and thriving in the unknown. I want to share an excerpt from Paul Tripp—pastor, event speaker, and a best-selling and award-winning author. On the Paul Tripp Ministries website, there are 4 tips focusing on using your gifts to get over a fear of the unknown. These tips were so profound that I wanted to share them in their entirety.

1. *When God sends us, He goes with us. The Great Commission is bracketed by two promises: divine power ("All authority") and divine presence ("I am with you always"). It doesn't matter what follows the command to "Go" because Jesus guarantees the impossibility of us ever being in a situation, location or relationship on our own.*

2. *God gifts those whom He sends. God is never a poor steward of the gifts that He blesses us with. He doesn't just bless us with gifts, but He also blesses us with specific opportunities where those gifts can be used.*

3. *God accompanies His call with His provision. I've said this many times: If God puts a Red Sea in front of you and He means for you to cross it, He'll build a bridge, send a boat, give you the ability to swim, or part the waters Himself. If He calls you to the other side, He'll make a way for you to get there!*

4. *God redeems our failures. Apart from our lack of sovereignty, we're also afraid of the unknown because we're afraid of us. I wish I could say that my ministry has been free from failure, but I can't, so it's not uncommon for us to shy away from opportunity because we're afraid to mess up again.*

MY PERSONAL FEAR ABOUT WRITING THIS BOOK

I wanted to end with this topic, fear of the unknown, because it encapsulates all of the previous fears that were discussed. If you are fearing relationships, it's because you don't know if the person will be good to you and so you put up a wall. If you are interviewing for a new job and have to sit in front of a team of interviewers, and you don't see anyone around the table that looks like you; a wall may go up. In many instances you don't know the back story of the individuals interviewing you, and you are now fearing *IF* they will look beyond your differences and treat you fairly. This is a prime example of a fear of the unknown wrapped in the idea of social inequality.

At times we give a fear of the unknown so much power over us. It can be like our kryptonite! Many things in this life that we want to do, we just didn't do because we didn't know what the end result would be. This concept is a representation of our lack of faith. Faith that God would not protect us, or give us the knowledge we need, or even the words to say. A lack of faith is like you giving others total control over your being. Visualize yourself dangling from strings being controlled by a puppetmaster. When you have faith, those strings don't exist! You are FREE—you can do as you please and experience things you never dreamt of.

During the process of writing this book, a wave of fear of the unknown took over me. I became afraid that if I released this book, I would get fired from my new position at Kent State University, or worse yet, get fired from the University as a whole. I began talking myself out of releasing the book. I kept asking myself, "Am I incriminating my university?" "Will the university not see the overall message in the text and decide that I no longer should be employed there?" I wasn't ready to give up my career with the university. As this wave of fear swept over me, in the back of my mind I was thinking to myself, "Well, I'm not gonna put the book out anyway, so why spend the time working on it?" My inner critic was starting to take control over me.

However, God really has a way of swinging open the doors when you are destined for greatness. Even in the bleakest moments, He will put a shine on your life that is an undeniable call to action. My favorite university president at Kent State retired in the summer of 2019. I was contacted by her assistant and was honored to find out that the President wanted me to come to an event and say a few words on her behalf. The day of the event came, and that evening I was so busy hustling to try to get things done and on top of that, I had to drive 30 minutes to get my boys from school and another 30 minutes back to the university for the celebration with my babies in tote. I emailed her assistant that I would be late, but I would be there. When I arrived, the event was well underway. I walked in about 25 minutes before I had to go up on stage! My time came, and I walked up on stage and was greeted by the university Provost. As I stood there in front of our university President and many community leaders including the mayor of Akron, I told my story.

Like many of us, my first encounter with President Beverly J. Warren was during her listening tour. With high enthusiasm she made her rounds to each and every department, school, division, and campus at Kent State University. However, my first personal encounter with President Warren was during the process of curating my (dis)ABLED BEAUTY Exhibition, which opened at the Kent State University Museum in fall 2016. It was a show that featured highly designed devices and clothes for those who were fashionable and just so happened to have a disability. I had contacted President Warren and asked her if she would be willing to allow me to feature the unique arm slings that the Fashion School had designed for her after she injured her arm. After a few days went by I received an email confirmation that yes, she was willing to allow me to use those arm slings for my show! And from then on, she and I began developing a friendship. And for the first time ever, I felt that I had a university president who was accessible and easy to talk to you. I've always been very comfortable approaching her to say hello and now every time I see her, we greet each other with a hug. Which is great, because I'm a hugger! I believe in showing love to everybody!

I have been at Kent State University for almost 15 years now. My journey is a bit unique in that I started off teaching in The Fashion School part time. while working in the industry as a Fashion Designer and starting my PhD journey. Once I had completed my coursework in 2008, I applied for an NTT instructor position in the Fashion School. And then once I completed my PhD in 2011, I went to JR Campbell who was the director at that time, and I expressed my concerns that the Fashion School has never had an African American Professor. I knew in my spirit that I was going to be the one and he could not have agreed more. Being the first African American professor has not been easy, but through hard work and grace, I made tenure and promotion. And not only did I make tenure and promotion, but I excelled at making tenure and promotion! In the words of my good friend Gregory King, "There's no other way but to slay!" Being the first required me to work hard, to exceed expectations and to blaze a trail for those coming behind me. My work received and continues to receive international recognition.

President Warren took notice and mentioned my work in her last State of the University address. Provost Diacon also noticed, and I was one of five faculty invited to dinner at the board of trustees banquet this past fall. During the banquet event, President Warren came up to me, she put her arms around me and told me how proud she was. She knew a bit about some of the struggles that I had endured becoming the first African American Professor in my school. After the hug President Warren looked me in the eyes, held my hands and gave me the most sincere congratulations. I will never forget it! (This is when the tears started flowing!) It was another confirmation for me that I can do anything in this life that I want despite what society says. A wise person once said, "success leaves foot prints," and mine left a helluva mark on Beverly Warren, Todd Diacon, John Crawford-Spinelli, and JR Campbell! I am so happy to say that as of Spring 2020, I will be serving as the new Associate Dean for the College of the Arts! President Warren, thank you soooo much for being a model of excellence for EVERYBODY and a caring heart to me as a growing academic and administrative professional. You will be missed!!

After I spoke at the retirement event, people were coming up to me, hugging me and telling me thank you. They were saying things like, "I really needed to hear that," or "Thank you for being so brave to speak your truth." A few days after the event, I received a beautiful email from an African American woman who is employed for the university.

Dear Dr. Ellington,

I heard you speak at President Warren's retirement celebration earlier this week and I would be remise if I did not reach out to you and share how your story impacted me. I'm sure we've probably crossed paths before, but I haven't had the pleasure of getting to know you personally. It is not often that we are empowered to share our stories in spaces like that, and far more uncommon to hear of our individual successes. Hearing you tell the real of your story as "the first," "the only" and the achievement you've had in being so with such grace and dignity, truly touched me as a young black woman who has been in spaces throughout my career dominated by those who do not look like me nor have shared similar lived experiences. When you teared up, I teared up. I was so proud for you and although you were sharing your own narrative you were a voice for those of us who were not on that stage and namely me. Thank you for being vulnerable in your remarks. I felt inspired and encouraged by what you shared. I also wanted to congratulate you on your promotion as Asst. Dean of College of the Arts (I think that was the title, but please correct me if I'm wrong)! All wonderful things you shared. All very much appreciated.

Her words gave me my SUPERPOWER!! And now here YOU are reading about my life!! The next story is about the life of an amazing young man whom I met during my travels.

THE PLANE RIDE OF A LIFETIME

Last summer I had the most amazing plane ride I ever had in my life! I was on my way back from conference in Scottsdale, Arizona. I had taken an Uber to get to the Phoenix airport and when I got there, since I had already checked in online all I needed to do was check in my bag. So, I go through the line, hand over my bag and head to security. I had enough time to go through security without much urgency. As a matter fact, this is one of the times that I can remember where I got to the airport very early and spent much of my time sitting and waiting at the gate for my departure. Usually, I'm rushing and stressing about missing my flight, this time was abnormally chill. As I was waiting at the gate, an announcement came over the overhead stating that my flight had been canceled due to mechanical issues, and the airline is going to be assisting patrons on finding an alternate flight. So, my hour wait time turned into a three-hour wait time.

Finally, the agent got on the overhead and made the announcement that we were going to begin boarding the plane in the next 15 minutes. Since I was flying Southwest, my fellow patrons and I started lining up according to our number placement. This boarding process is somewhat agitating because you never know if you're in the right order unless you asked the person in front of you and behind you what their number is. A young African American man steps up to the line, and just like everyone else, he is trying to figure out his boarding position. His number was after mine, but I decided to let him go in front of me because he had on a pair of sneakers embellished with hand graffiti, and I wanted to have the opportunity to admire his kicks! So, he jumps in front of me and I start engaging him in conversation about his sneakers.

He goes on to tell me that he has a good friend who is a graffiti artist, and the guy embellishes shoes and accessories for a living. I told him about my pair of off-white Keds that I embellished with a black sharpie inspired by the Malian textile mud cloth. My hand-made mud-cloth-drawn shoes had nothing on the elaborate graffiti on his shoes. As the conversation goes on, I could tell that the young man was from the inner-city of Phoenix. Being raised in the inner city, I can often tell when someone has a similar background just by their body stance and their speech patterns. During the conversation, I found out that he was interested in fashion and eventually aspired to have his own business. I told him that I was a professor of fashion and our conversation picked up more momentum from there.

The agent gets back on the overhead for the third and final time and begins scanning boarding passes as patrons begin shuffling through the line. All of a sudden, the young man turns around towards me and says he made a mistake and he's not going fly today. He had a look of panic on his face, and I asked what was going on. He revealed to me that he was afraid of flying. He was on his way to his cousin's wedding several states over, and this would be his first time on a plane. I politely, but physically, turned him around and talked him through the process as we continued to shuffle through the line. As we began walking down the aisle of the plane, his anxiety kicked up another notch. He grabbed my hand and said, "you can't leave me." I told him that I would ask whomever was sitting next to him if I could switch seats. So, as we get closer to his seat, a middle-age guy was sitting in the seat next to where the one the young man was assigned to. I politely asked (with a little white lie), "Hi sir, do you mind if I switch seats with you so that I can sit next to my son?" He graciously got up and I allowed the young man to sit down in the middle seat while I sat on the aisle seat.

As soon as his rear end touched the seat, his anxiety went up again. At this point, he was shaking and almost in tears. There was a lady sitting at the window in our row, and she noticed what was going on. Luckily, she was an off-duty flight attendant on her way home from her shift. She gave the young man some encouraging words and some tactics to help him relax. As the flight attendant working on that aircraft made the announcement that the doors were closing and we would be pushing off soon, the young man's anxiety went up another notch! He now was holding my hand and the hand of the off-duty flight attendant.

The plane slowly pulled out of its parked position at the gate and began coasting down the runway. As soon as the wheels lifted off the ground, this young man gripped both our hands tight and the tears started streaming down his face. The takeoff was a little bumpy, but I could not show my bit of angst because that would've made the situation worse! As the plane continued to rise higher to reach its altitude, he continued to hold our hands and the tears continue to fall down his face. I had just remembered that I have brought some fashion magazines with me, so I pulled those out of my bag and begin sharing those with the young man. I wanted to keep talking to him in order to help him relax. I began going into more depth about what I do as a fashion professor, creating designs and attending exhibitions. The plane finally reached altitude and the pressure on my hand began to ease up a bit. I continued to keep him engaged in conversation and he was able to get through the flight in a more relaxed state.

When we reached our destination, I had a unique layover; one that did not require that I leave the plane. I explained to the young man that I was staying on the plane. He gave me an unnerved stare along with puppy dog eyes as if to say, "Please don't leave me!" The off-duty flight attendant grabbed his hand and promised me that she would get him to his next fight. I pulled out my business card, gave it to him and told him he could call me anytime. As he shuffled down the aisle of the plane for the last time, he looked back at me and gave me a smile, a reassuring smile to show me that he would be OK! I watched him walk off the plane and as soon as I saw that he was out of my sight, the tears started streaming down MY face! I started thanking God that he gave me the opportunity to be present for that young man. Without my original flight getting canceled due to mechanical issues, I would never have been there. God is so amazing that he puts people in our lives for the most awesome reasons. I got the honor of witnessing this young man successfully face his fears. A few weeks later, he called me up. The first thing he said when we spoke is, "I made it to my cousin's wedding! It was beautiful and I was so happy to see my family. Thank you again for everything you did."

Having a fear of the unknown can be a very unsettling feeling! However, once you get over that fear, the feeling that you get from accomplishing your fear is INDESCRIBABLE! Young man, if you were reading this, just know that you have inspired me as much as or even more than I have inspired you. Keep pushing yourself into the unknown and continue to come out on the other side of greatness! XOXO

THE FINAL HOUR IS NOW!

9 HEROIC STRATEGIES TO IGNITE THE BEST VERSION OF YOU

#1 YOUR VOICE COMES FROM GOD, YOUR FEAR COME FROM THE DEVIL

Remember what you have to say matters to the world. In order to demolish fear of your voice, you have to break it down, deconstruct it, and turn it into dust. Demolishing fear also means that you defeated it. You didn't allow it to catch you and get the best of you. Fear gets no goals, no baskets, and no touchdowns over you! Once you destroy fear you can do your victory dance all over its head. Once you utterly ruin fear, you can speak your testimony from the roof tops, while your creator smiles down at you!! Isaiah 43:1 puts it plainly, "don't fear for I have redeemed you; I have called you by name; you are mine." What God is saying here is that there's no reason to have fear in your spirit. Your spirit belongs to God and he has given you every tool that you need to be successful in this life. No matter how hard times get, you must always understand that you have a way out. God always has your back, your front *and* your sides. NONE of the success that I have had thus far in my life was done alone. I pray for creativity, I pray for strength, I pray for patience, I pray for grace. God gives me all of those and more.

Fear is the devil's work. According to the a 2016 Huffpost article, *"Top 5 scriptures that banish fear,"* God purposefully speaks about fear as a state of mind that we should not wallow in. The phrase, "fear not" is used at least 80 times in the Bible, most likely because God knows the enemy uses fear to decrease our hope and limit our victories. When we allow negative spirits and negative people to diminish our dreams, that is a message to God that from the beginning, we did not have hope OR faith.

#2 USE PUBLIC SPEAKING AS A PLATFORM FOR YOUR SUCCESS AND TO SERVICE OTHERS

Mastering public speaking is not easy. It is really truly all about confidence and preparedness. According to Virtual Speech, the benefits of being able to speak in public is critical in "building personal development on many levels, since improving communication skills is helpful in almost every area of life." Being afraid to speak in public also limits the opportunities for sharing your talents and knowledge with others. I believe that it is truly a sin not to use the gifts that God gave you to better the world. No matter what your line of work is, always think about the impact that you are having on the world. Think about the youth who are watching you; you are a role model to someone, even if you don't know it. Someone is modeling their life after you, thus it is your responsibility to live the best life that you can, so that those coming after you will have you as a positive example. If you can't become better at public speaking for yourself, think about all those people who NEED to hear what you have to say in order to enhance their way of knowing and being.

"The best way to find yourself is to lose yourself in the service of others."

-Mahatma Gandhi.

#3 REALTIONSHIPS ARE NECESSARY—BUT BE STRATEGIC ABOUT WHO YOU LET IN YOUR CIRCLE

One of the best things you can do for yourself is to DROP the laggards and blood suckers in your life. My BFF, who I talked about earlier, was like my sister but I had to remove her from my immediate circle because she was waiting for me to fail so that she could have a reason to feel better about her lack of accomplishment. Having to cut her out of my life hurt like HELL! I wish I could have brought her along with me on my journey to abundance. But know, becoming the best you can be is not for the faint of heart.

You can't be fearful that God won't supply you with worthy friendships of likeminded people as you climb the ladder to success.

That was a fear I most certainly had to get over, and one that I still struggle with today. Networking with others doing similar things with their life is a great way to combat that fear. Always remember, what you give off, you will get back. You may have heard of the phrase, "If you know and hang out with 9 broke people, you will be the 10th." Or, "You are the sum of the 5 closest people you spend the most time with," says speaker and entrepreneur Jim Rohn. In other words, "birds of a feather flock together." If you are a good friend, you will attract good people. If you strive for success and excellence, those same type of people will find their way into your life. It's just the way the universe works.

#4 UNDERSTAND THAT GOD MADE US ALL EQUAL, AND WE ALL HAVE THE SAME OPPORTUNITIES—"MAKE IT HAPPEN" (IN MY MARIAH CAREY VOICE)!

Gary Zukav, American spiritual teacher and author of four consecutive New York Times best sellers, discussed his definition of spiritual partnership during Orpah's Super Soul Sunday podcast. One major component to having a spiritual partnership with others is the raw and eternal belief that everyone in this life is equal. Mr. Zukav stated that, "Equality is understanding that there is nothing and

no one in the universe more or less important than you. If
you don't feel equal, you will feel either superiority or
inferiority. Feelings of superiority or inferiority are
personality traits that emerge from fear." DEEP!!!

The famous quote, "the only thing we have to fear, is
fear itself," was declared by our President Franklin D.
Roosevelt. This was his self-testimony! He successfully
served as President for 12 years as a wheelchair user (yes,
that's 3 terms—before the 2-term law went into effect in
1951). FDR was diagnosed with polio in his late 30s and
never recovered his full ability to walk. That did not stop
him in the least. He was a fearless leader in many ways!
However, he still had some fears of his own. He and his
staff remarkably hid his disability for most of his
presidency. FDR's fear of societal inequality led him to
believe that the American people would not accept a
disabled person as their president. Even with that obstacle,
he was able to make fear his SUPERPOWER and serve the
Presidency regardless of his condition or how others might
perceive him. Research shows that people with disabilities
are often viewed by society as less able, less social, less
intelligent, and even less beautiful than able-bodied people.
FDR was able to deconstruct and destroy the shame that
society places on those who have a disability. I can just
image the guts it took to do that!

One of the most courageous people of our time was
Harriet Tubman. She too had a physical handicap, which
resulted from a blow to her head, but that did not keep her
from helping more than 300 enslaved people escape to

freedom. Tubman must have been knowledgeable of the concept of the body controlling the mind; because during the trek from the south to the north, some enslaved people would get afraid and want to turn back. She would pull out her rifle, point it at those who were wanting to turn back and say with power, "You'll be free or die a slave!" With the help of a spiritual connection with the universe, in our greatest weaknesses, we can find a strength and courage we never knew we had. Harriet Tubman knew the calling on her life. She knew that her God would always be with her. Through her journeys from the South to the North and back, she led her sister, brother, and her nieces to freedom. On her third journey to the South, she went to collect her husband, only to find out that he had married another woman. Heartbreak, fear, and regret did not hinder her from making more than 15 more trips back to the South to help guide others to freedom. Again, at our weakest moments we can find our SUPERPOWER! I am proof! Let fear be your INVIGORATOR, not your DEBILIATOR!

I had the privilege of getting a personal tour of Mrs. Tubman's house in Auburn, New York. I was amazed as I walked into the house, which had been immaculately restored. The home had many rooms and surprisingly it had a second floor which was just a beautiful as the first floor. As I walked through the home that once belonged to Mrs. Tubman, an immense feeling of strength came over me. If a former slave can work hard and earn an abundant life, I sure as hell can!

#5 BASKE IN YOUR OWN BEAUTY, DON'T ALLOW SOCIETY TO MAKE YOU FEEL INFERIOR

All people, all women, but my Black Sisters, especially… know that you were created EXACTLY as God saw fit! As George Fraser stated, "Black people…we were the first!" For millions of years we ruled over the earth, and the definition of beauty was a representation of our Black skin and kinky hair. Lighter skin tones did not appear on earth until 7,000-8,000 years ago. I say this again to say, White skin is not the measure of all things beautiful. Black women, you are not inferior. Black men, Black women are not inferior; therefore, we need you to see and appreciate our beauty.

Race and skin tone aside, true beauty comes in the form of divine love which asks, "How can I serve others?" There are many women who society would classify as being "amazingly beautiful," but they can be some of the most miserable, vindictive people on the planet because many times being "amazingly beautiful" comes coupled with being self-centered and egotistical. In this way, it is utterly impossible to operate from a place of divine love. In everything you do, seek beauty and grace and ask yourself, "Am I operating from my lower self (ego) or from my higher self (divine love)? When you die, your eulogy will not discuss how physically beautiful you were, but how beautiful your spirit was and how you served many people.

I'm a fashion designer by trade—beauty and aesthetics are my everyday life; however, when I die and I attend my funeral in my spiritual form wearing the gold and white cloak that my creator draped around my shoulders, I want to see the venue so stacked with people that many have to stand, and I want to hear how I touched and added substance to the lives of everyone that I encountered.

#6 USE YOUR VULERABILITY AS A STENGTH INSEAD OF AS A WEAKNESS

Having the strength to reveal your vulnerability to others is a grand gesture in God's trust. It is a shining example of what is means to be selfless and to only seek growth and service in your life. It's easy to say and much harder to do, but the first step is taking the ego out of it. Jesus Christ stated during the Last Supper, "I have given you an example that you should do as I have done to you," (John 13:15), after the act of washing the feet of all his disciples. We are meant to be in the world as helpmates to each other. Vulnerability is to the benefit to the ENTIRE human race; it will bring us closer together and make us more harmonious in our overall life. Dr. Brené Brown stated that, "Vulnerability sounds like truth and feels like courage."

#7 WE ARE HUMAN, WE ALL MAKE MISTAKES—ALLOW YOURSELF ROOM TO FAIL, IT JUST INDICATES THAT YOU ARE GROWING

Society doesn't have to shame us because we often times will shame ourselves by getting caught up in the fear of making a mistake and being humiliated. On one episode of the *Willie Jolley Wealthy Ways* podcast, Dr. Jolley talks about our need to stop shaming ourselves and be our own role model. If you need something, you have to ask for it! You can't be ashamed! People can't read your mind! As the saying goes, "A closed mouth doesn't get fed." You can't be afraid to ask for what you want. Asking questions is not a sign of weakness, but an indicator of your willingness to grow.

My fellow Clevelander and Kent State Golden Flash, Steve Harvey stated that, "The best things in life are on the opposite ends of fear!" Anything in this life that you want to achieve, comes with taking risks. For many years I smothered and hid my entrepreneurial spirit because I was too afraid to break out and start my own business. I had no examples of any one I was close to who had a business, so I had no models. Some people are blessed to grow up around their family business, but just because you don't come from an entrepreneurial family, does not mean you can't be successful in business for yourself. It's all about your desire, drive, and your vulnerability in asking for help. I stopped worrying about my potential mistakes or failures and started thinking about all the people who would miss out on what I have to offer the world if I didn't start my business. Entrepreneur and author Diane F. Smith says that we should "Find the lesson in failure, first by recognizing that it is a learning experience. Then acknowledge that it was supposed to happen because all experiences come from the Universe." God has your back; all happens exactly the way it should! Failures are inevitable, you can't stop them. Well, maybe you can, if you never try anything new.

#8 ALWAYS AIM FOR EXCELLENCE, IT WILL BRING YOU MUCH SUCCESS AND WILL HELP YOU BE EXCITED FOR OTHERS' SUCCESSES

Stop being like everybody else! In the world of fashion, looking like everybody else is a no-no! Who wants to be a copycat or a knockoff? Have you ever gone to a party or other social event and noticed that someone was wearing the exact same outfit as you! I *despise* looking like, acting like, and dressing like anyone.

Dennis S Brown, motivational speaker and author of the book *Change Your Attitude, Change Your Life* says, "Sometimes you have to walk OUTSIDE the circle!" Your attitude about your circumstances can make or break you. I truly believe that much of my success stemmed from my desire to have an attitude of excellence, which was far different than anyone else around me. In my inner-city neighborhood, I was an anomaly. There were not many people who were working toward their greatness, instead they were often wallowing in the fact that they were poor, uneducated, and descendants of slaves. They gave up their power based on the simple fact that society had not been kind to them. Attitude is all in the mind!

Even if you don't believe in God, there is no denying the universal laws that exists in our world. The universal law of correspondence is the basis for the natural reciprocating cycle of what you put out is what you get back. Your energy will match the energy that's coming back to you. If you are fearful, and your thoughts are profound in fear, this is the only type of energy that will come back to you. If you are hating on people because they have achieved great things in their lives, that "hateration" will surely circle back to you. The universe can't give you something that you have not earned. Positive thoughts of excellence will lead to your positive actions and behaviors, which then show up in the excellence of your work—work that others are blessed to witness. Fearful thoughts lead to fearful actions and behaviors, which often translates into being stagnant in your career, being lonely in your relationships, and wishing ill to those you envy.

You can only be blessed if you bless others. You can only be successful if you have BELIEF in your POTENTIAL! Tony Robbins, entrepreneur, author and motivator extraordinaire, talks about something he calls "The Success Cycle."

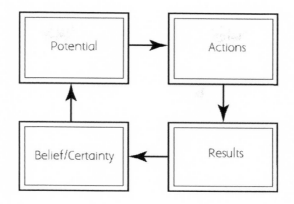

Robbin's Success Cycle is a simplified explanation of Merton's Self-fulfilling Prophecy theory. YOUR perceptions of YOU are far greater than OTHERS' perceptions of you. First off, you can control how you feel about yourself. You can NOT control how others feel about you (even though I know sometimes we wish we could). Your level of success will depend solely on your belief and certainty of your potential to accomplish whichever goal you set forth. Whatever level of potential you feel you have will be a direct representation of the action that you put toward your goals. Your level of action will be a direct representation of the level of results or outcomes that you get. You know how they say, "you get what you put in." If you put in half-ass action because you don't truly believe that you are capable or have the capacity for a certain goal—you will get half-ass results. Plain and simple! Much of knowing your potential comes from you knowing WHO you are and WHY you are in this life. It is a journey, but once you figure it out, man…. "it's on like popcorn!" LOL!

#9 NO ONE KNOWS EVERYTHING; THIS LIFE IS A CONTINUAL JOURNEY OF THE UNKNOWN—EXPLORE AND BE GLAD IN THE MYSTERY!

Andrew Morrison, marketing heavy weight and multi-millionaire entrepreneur, stated something that has stuck with me since I listened to him (for the 100th time) on the podcast hosted by Brother Bedford—*Conversations with Black Millionaire Entrepreneurs.*

> *"If I can help people begin their day by doing nothing. If I can help people begin their day by being silent. The whole world is impacting you. The whole world is trying to tell you how to act, what to think and what to do. I'm telling you, the reason why you are stuck right now and the reason why somebody can't find a way out is because they have not become STILL. So, I want everyone to begin to have a practice—a daily practice of stillness. Give yourself 15 minutes first thing in the morning and 15 minutes before you go to bed. Just sit there and do NOTHING—sit there and be STILL and remember your CALLING! Remember who you are! You can face any tragedy, any obstacle in life if you know who you are! Many folks go through life disconnected from their divine power source. You don't know who you are, who don't know WHOSE you are, nor do you know who sent you! And so,*

when you see someone doing "great things," it's
because they know why they are SENT!

-Andrew Morrison

Deep… truths! So, who are you? I know who I am, and I am still in the process of learning what I am sent here to become. It's a constant soul search to fight to be fearless and to be better than I was the day before.

Your fearfulness can be erased—can be demolished by meditating and clearing your mind. Connecting with the Alpha-Theta state of your mind can relieve stress, anxiety, heartbreaks and all other issues you may have in life. Mindvalley, an organization that focuses on healing the mind, body, and spirit of its clients, discusses that our Alpha-Theta brain waves are where the optimal range for visualization, mind programming, and using the brains creative power begins. Alpha-Theta is where you consciously create your reality. Did you just read that?? YOU **consciously create** YOUR REALITY!

We can conceive ourselves to be whatever we wish! WE have the POWER, RESOURCEFULNESS and COURAGE to develop our lives into what we dream about. God wants abundance for us—prosperity, love, and peace of mind. I know I want abundance in my life! I am still on that journey of learning how to deeply connect with the universe and my "infinite intelligence," as author of *Think and Grow Rich*, Napoleon Hill puts it. I can honestly say that every major goal in my life that I have set after, I have achieved. I believe speaking my desires into the universe will allow my God to connect me with the right people and resources I need to make that happen. This is not to say that you can snap your fingers, and everything will be given unto you, because it won't. God has done His part, and He EXPECTS that you will do yours. Remember… "God helps those who help themselves." Mediation has begun to make a great change in my life, just knowing that I have one space and a single time continuum where I am no one but me. Not a wife, a mother, sister, friend, daughter or educator. At that moment as I listen to my slow breaths moving inward and outward—filling my body, and then emptying from my body; I am no one but my creator's child. I was born from the same earth and seas of our natural world, and so were you! My creator blew breathe into me and he blew breathe into you. The universe is waiting to reconnect with you. What are you waiting for? Don't let your fear DEBILITATE you.

Dr. Joe Dispenza, international lecturer, researcher, corporate consultant, author, and educator gave a lecture on Tom Bilyeu's Impact Theory platform entitled *Learn How to Control Your Mind.* He discussed that our body is our unconscious mind and the hardest part about advancing in this life is not necessarily changing your mind or attitude, but also getting your body to react to your new way of thinking. When we do something or react to thinking in the same way over and over again, our body gets conditioned to behaving in a certain manner. When we step outside of our norm and do something different, we begin to feel uncomfortable. Due to the uncomfortable state we are in, our body wants to return to the familiar territory and react like it would have in the past. In this way, the body is the leader and the mind is *not* in control! Dr. Joe continues that, being in the unknown is a scary place because it's unpredictable! The best way to handle the unknown is to control it and create your destiny! At every cost, even if you have to force people along with a rifle, like our sister Harriet did!

Alexander the Great—whether he was a great man or not, that has been up for debate; however, when he stated, "Each moment free from fear makes a man immortal!" He staked his claim in that fear *can* become one's SUPERPOWER! If you allow fear to eat you alive or if you use it as fuel, this decision will determine if you have what it takes to use fear as your FIRE instead of as an EXTINGUISHER to your greatness. I'm on FIRE!! How about YOU?!

Do you have the AUDACITY to beat your fear? What is your motivation?? Do you want a better life? One that you could not have even dreamt up! Do you believe that you are worthy? Bury your fear under HOPE *and* FAITH! Get pumped up about the possibilities that await you in the next phase of your life! "Fear is not a proper motivator," Michelle Obama reminds us. "Hope wins out." In the spirt of Mrs. Obama, let HOPE *and* FAITH be the antidote to your fear. God's LOVE and GRACE can carry you to unimaginable places. Again, I am a PERFECT example of what God's love can do! "Perfect love casts out all fear" (John 4:18). Erykah Badu was right! Fear and love don't mix!

CLAIM, BELIEVE, WAIT! CLAIM your courage and strength! Truly BELIEVE that you can do anything! That need, want or desire in your life is coming! WAIT, it's on its way—the universe WILL deliver! As long as you do those things, in that order, with unwavering HOPE *and* FAITH, your SUPERPOWERS will arise!

Tameka Ellington
October 20, 2018 · 🌐 ▾

•••

These are the eyes of a first generation revolutionary. A futurist, a resilient, powerful, beautifully intelligent woman who is determined to break the cycle of poverty. I am the first African American Professor of the Kent State University Fashion School. This honor came with much reward as well as much strife. I am ecstatic to say that my creator gave me the audacity to catapult over those inequities before me. I rose like a phoenix from her ashes, and I am still on fire!! I am so proud to say that I have been given the extraordinary opportunity to be named the new Associate Dean for the Kent State University College of the Arts!! There is NOTHING I can't do with my creator guiding my steps and my family by my side. If you are a first generation revolutionary, let me get a HELL YEAH!

⭕👍💗 191   130 Comments 6 Shares

D r. Tameka N. Ellington is a First-Generation Revolutionary, Scholar, Educator, Speaker, Image Specialist and Philanthropist. She is Founder and CEO of Entirely Incorporated, a multidimensional human wellness business with the goal of helping clients live their full life. She is extremely passionate about youth and young adult development and the empowerment of those who are first generation. Dr. Tameka is CEO/Founder of The First-Generation Revolutionaries Movement™, a campaign to equip future revolutionaries with professional advancement, spiritual fulfillment, mentorship, authentic camaraderie and networking. She specializes in self-empowerment, professional development, as well as social and professional dress etiquette. Dr. Tameka's purpose in life is to help others turn their fears into useful strategies for an abundant life.

Book Dr. Tameka
to facilitate a workshop and/or speak at your next event!
info@drtamekaellington.com
440-427-4813
Social Media

Made in the USA
Middletown, DE
28 March 2022